Clear**Revise**

AQA GCSE
Business

Illustrated revision and practice

Published by
PG Online Limited
The Old Coach House
35 Main Road
Tolpuddle
Dorset
DT2 7EW
United Kingdom

sales@pgonline.co.uk
www.clearrevise.com
www.pgonline.co.uk
2024

PREFACE

Absolute clarity! That's the aim.

This is everything you need to ace the examined component in this course and beam with pride. Each topic is laid out in a beautifully illustrated format that is clear, approachable and as concise and simple as possible.

Each section of the specification is clearly indicated to help you cross-reference your revision. The checklist on the contents pages will help you keep track of what you have already worked through and what's left before the big day.

We have included worked exam-style questions with answers for almost every topic. This helps you understand where marks are coming from and to see the theory at work for yourself in an exam situation. There is also a set of exam-style questions at the end of each section for you to practise writing answers for. You can check your answers against those given at the end of the book.

LEVELS OF LEARNING

Based on the degree to which you are able to truly understand a new topic, we recommend that you work in stages. Start by reading a short explanation of something, then try and recall what you've just read. This has limited effect if you stop there but it aids the next stage. Question everything. Write down your own summary and then complete and mark a related exam-style question. Cover up the answers if necessary but learn from them once you've seen them. Lastly, teach someone else. Explain the topic in a way that they can understand. Have a go at the different practice questions – they offer an insight into how and where marks are awarded.

Design and artwork: Jessica Webb / PG Online Ltd
Airport image © Sorbis / Shutterstock.com

First edition 2024   10 9 8 7 6 5 4 3 2 1
A catalogue entry for this book is available from the British Library
ISBN: 978-1-916518-11-7
Contributor: Paul Clark
Copyright © PG Online 2024
All rights reserved

This product is made of material from well-managed FSC®-certified forests and from recycled materials.
Printed by Bell & Bain Ltd, Glasgow, UK.

THE SCIENCE OF REVISION

Illustrations and words

Research has shown that revising with words and pictures doubles the quality of responses by students.[1] This is known as 'dual-coding' because it provides two ways of fetching the information from our brain. The improvement in responses is particularly apparent in students when they are asked to apply their knowledge to different problems. Recall, application and judgement are all specifically and carefully assessed in public examination questions.

Retrieval of information

Retrieval practice encourages students to come up with answers to questions.[2] The closer the question is to one you might see in a real examination, the better. Also, the closer the environment in which a student revises is to the 'examination environment', the better. Students who had a forthcoming test 2–7 days away did 30% better using retrieval practice than students who simply read, or repeatedly reread material. Students who were expected to teach the content to someone else after their revision period did better still.[3] What was found to be most interesting in other studies is that students using retrieval methods and testing for revision were also more resilient to the introduction of stress.[4]

Ebbinghaus' forgetting curve and spaced learning

Ebbinghaus' 140-year-old study examined the rate at which we forget things over time. The findings still hold true. However, the act of forgetting facts and techniques and relearning them is what cements them into the brain.[5] Spacing out revision is more effective than cramming – we know that, but students should also know that the space between revisiting material should vary depending on how far away the examination is. A cyclical approach is required. An examination 12 months away necessitates revisiting covered material about once a month. A test in 30 days should have topics revisited every 3 days – intervals of roughly a tenth of the time available.[6]

Summary

Students: the more tests and past questions you do, in an environment as close to examination conditions as possible, the better you are likely to perform on the day. If you prefer to listen to music while you revise, tunes without lyrics will be far less detrimental to your memory and retention. Silence is most effective.[5] If you choose to study with friends, choose carefully – effort is contagious.[7]

1. Mayer, R. E., & Anderson, R. B. (1991). Animations need narrations: An experimental test of dual-coding hypothesis. *Journal of Education Psychology*, (83)4, 484–490.

2. Roediger III, H. L., & Karpicke, J.D. (2006). Test-enhanced learning: Taking memory tests improves long-term retention. *Psychological Science*, 17(3), 249–255.

3. Nestojko, J., Bui, D., Kornell, N. & Bjork, E. (2014). Expecting to teach enhances learning and organisation of knowledge in free recall of text passages. *Memory and Cognition*, 42(7), 1038–1048.

4. Smith, A. M., Floerke, V. A., & Thomas, A. K. (2016) Retrieval practice protects memory against acute stress. *Science*, 354(6315), 1046–1048.

5. Perham, N., & Currie, H. (2014). Does listening to preferred music improve comprehension performance? *Applied Cognitive Psychology*, 28(2), 279–284.

6. Cepeda, N. J., Vul, E., Rohrer, D., Wixted, J. T. & Pashler, H. (2008). Spacing effects in learning a temporal ridgeline of optimal retention. *Psychological Science*, 19(11), 1095–1102.

7. Busch, B. & Watson, E. (2019), *The Science of Learning*, 1st ed. Routledge.

CONTENTS

MARK ALLOCATIONS

Green mark allocations *[1]* on answers to in-text questions throughout this guide help to indicate where marks are gained within the answers. A bracketed '1' e.g. *[1]* = one valid point worthy of a mark. In longer answer questions, a mark is given based on the whole response. In these answers, a tick mark *[✓]* indicates that a valid point has been made. There are often many more points to make than there are marks available so you have more opportunity to max out your answers than you may think.

COMMAND VERBS

Points-based questions

Calculate

Calculation questions will be worth 2–5 marks, depending on the number of steps you need to do to get to the final answer. You do not get any marks for simply writing the formula unless the question specifically states this. A correct answer will always score full marks, but ensure you show your working out as a backup. If your answer is incorrect, you may get some marks for correct workings. If the question asks for 1 or 2 decimal places, make sure you reflect this in your answer, or you will lose a mark.

Explain

There are two types of 'Explain' questions. They will be either worth 2 or 4 marks. The 2-mark questions are points based. The 4-mark questions are levels based. 4-mark questions will ask you to explain an impact, benefit, drawback or method. For the 2 mark 'Explain' questions, you will need to make a valid point and then support it with a linked strand of development. To do this, you need to use clear connectives such as 'therefore', 'this leads to', 'because', 'so' and 'as a result'. Try to avoid the use of the word 'also' as this indicates you are moving onto a second point.

Sometimes you will be asked to 'Identify and explain two benefits, drawbacks or impacts'. For these questions, do as you would for a 2-mark 'Explain' question, but do it twice. See it as 2 × 2 mark 'Explain questions'.

Define, describe or what is meant by

These questions require you to give the meaning of a word or phrase.

Give, identify, list or state

These questions involve a short response to name or characterise something.

Levels-based questions

Explain

4-mark 'Explain' questions are contextualised. These questions will follow on from a case study. For these you must provide a valid point, benefit or drawback and then have three linked strands of development.

You will also need to include application in your response, making your answer specific to the business presented in the case study.

Analyse

Analyse questions carry 6 marks. To answer effectively, either develop one point with at least five linked strands, or make two points in separate paragraphs, ensuring at least five strands between them. No marks are given for evaluation, so if asked to analyse benefits, discuss only one or two advantages. Mentioning drawbacks would be invalid unless the question specifically asks about impacts. Additionally, these questions assess application, so tailor your response to the specific business in the case study.

Recommend

These questions will be worth 9 marks. The question will ask you to recommend whether a business should take a certain course of action. In answering these questions, you should adopt a three-paragraph approach:

Paragraph 1: State the benefit of the topic presented in the question. You should analyse the point you have made by developing it using connectives. Aim to have at least three linked strands of development. The question tests application as well. Therefore, your paragraph should be relevant and specific about the business in the case study.

Paragraph 2: Give a counter argument by recognising a drawback. Again, support your point with at least three linked strands of development. Like the first paragraph, application is needed here.

Paragraph 3: This should be your conclusion and should be in the context of the business. Do you recommend they take that course of action? What are the key points that have led you to that decision? One way you can show high level evaluative skills is to use the 'it depends on...' rule. What might your final decision depend on?

Evaluate

These questions involve making a choice between two options. You should consider both options in your answer. When answering an evaluation question, you should also adopt a three-paragraph approach, all of which should be applied to the business in the case study:

Paragraph 1: Explain the benefits and drawbacks of the first option, using clear connectives.

Paragraph 2: Explain the benefits and drawbacks of the second option, using clear connectives.

Paragraph 3: This should be your conclusion and should be in the context of the business. What is the best option and why is it the best option for the business in the case study? What are the key points that have led you to that decision? Again, you can show high level evaluative skills by using the 'it depends on...' rule. What might your final decision depend on?

TOPICS FOR PAPERS 1 AND 2

Information about the papers

Specification coverage

Paper 1 covers sections 3.1, 3.2, 3.3 and 3.4.
Paper 2 covers sections 3.1, 3.2, 3.5 and 3.6.

Assessment

Written exams: Each 1 hour 45 minutes

Each paper is worth 90 marks

All questions are mandatory

Each paper is 50% of the qualification grade

Calculators are permitted.

Assessment overview

Each paper is divided into **three** sections:

Section A has multiple choice questions and short answer questions worth 20 marks.

Section B has one case study/data response stimuli with questions worth approximately 34 marks.

Section C has one case study/data response stimuli with questions worth approximately 36 marks.

THE PURPOSE AND NATURE OF BUSINESS

The **purpose of a business** is to produce a **good** or provide a **service**, these are collectively known as **products**.

Reasons for starting a business

A business is an organisation that provides a product to its customers. A business will be started for the following reasons:

 To produce goods

 To supply services

 To distribute products

 To fulfil a business opportunity

 To provide a good or service to benefit others

Goods, services, needs and wants

Goods are physical products, such as a car or a hairbrush, produced from raw materials for sale to businesses or consumers. A **service** is an action that is carried out to fulfil a need or demand in return for payment. Services are intangible (cannot be touched) and include buying insurance or a taxi ride.

Products are sold to **customers** (individuals, businesses or organisations who *buy* the products or make decision about which suppliers to use) so that they can be used by **consumers** (people who *use* the products). A business will be successful if it meets the needs and wants of customers.

The **wants** and **needs** of customers are constantly changing. Businesses must adapt their products in line with demand to ensure they are meeting these needs, and to prevent customers going to competitors.

Explain, using an example, the difference between a want and a need. [2]

A need is a basic human requirement whereas a want is the desire for a particular product.[1] For example there is a need for clothing, but customers will want the latest fashion item.[1]

Basic functions and types of business

Factors of production

In order to produce products, a business will need to use resources called factors of production. These include:

Land

The physical site that a business is located on, but this also includes the natural resources that the business uses in producing the good or in providing the service.

Capital investment

Machinery, equipment, buildings and vehicles used in production.

Enterprise

The skills of the people running the business to identify business opportunities. They also manage all the resources so that a business can meet the customers' needs and wants.

Labour

The number of people that are employed by a business and the skills that they possess.

Types of business

Primary industry

Primary sector businesses are those that extract Earth's natural resources from the ground. Examples include an oil company, a farmer or a coal mining business.

Secondary industry

A **secondary sector** business is one that turns raw materials into finished products. Examples of these would include a car manufacturer, or a business that manufactures mobile phones.

Tertiary industry

The **tertiary sector** includes businesses that provide a service to consumers or other businesses. These include takeaway delivery firms, hairdressers and cinemas.

BUSINESS ENTERPRISE AND ENTREPRENEURSHIP

An **enterprise** is a business that has the ability to identify a business idea and can take a risk in seeing that the idea is brought to market.

An **entrepreneur** is someone who starts and runs their own business. In doing so, the entrepreneur needs to demonstrate the necessary skills to be successful.

Objectives of an entrepreneur

There are many reasons why an entrepreneur may want to start their own business.

- To be their own boss – Business owners take control over their own working life and make all the decisions.
- Flexible working hours – Being an entrepreneur sometimes means being able to choose the working hours that suit them best.
- To pursue an interest – It is the objective of some entrepreneurs to run a business in an area that interests them. This helps them to achieve happiness and satisfaction from running a business in a sector that they have a passion for.
- To earn more money – Some entrepreneurs set up their own business so that they can make more money than they earned working for another business.
- To fulfil a gap in the market – An entrepreneur may want to start a business because they realise that no other business is meeting the needs and wants of potential customers, and they are confident that they could provide a better offer.
- Dissatisfaction with their current job – An entrepreneur may set up a business because they are unhappy in their current employment and need to make a change.

Explain **two** characteristics that are important for an entrepreneur to possess. [4]

Being organised.[1] Entrepreneurs must manage many resources effectively such as employees and suppliers.[1] A willingness to take risks.[1] Running a business is risky so an entrepreneur must be able to acknowledge and evaluate these risks.[1]
Other potential characteristics are being hard-working[1] and being innovative.[1]

Opportunity cost

Opportunity cost is the cost of making one choice at the expense of another, in terms of the use of limited resources. For example, a factory producing sweets has enough finance either for a new packing machine or to purchase a new fleet of delivery vehicles. If it chooses the packing machine, the opportunity cost becomes the value of the delivery vehicles to the business and the benefits these would bring that have been sacrificed.

THE DYNAMIC NATURE OF BUSINESS

Businesses operate in dynamic markets, meaning that they have to cope with an ever-changing environment.

Factors of change

Changes in business occur due to changes in **technology**, the **economic situation**, **legislation** and **environmental expectations** (these are covered in more detail in **section 3.2**). To be successful, businesses must have an appreciation of these changes and develop or adapt products to meet these needs. This can lead to new business ideas and opportunities.

Changes in technology

Technology develops at a rapid rate which regularly opens up new opportunities for businesses in terms of the products that they can provide and how products are produced. It has also changed the way that consumers shop, with many turning to e-commerce.

Legislation

New laws may be introduced that impact on the products that a business sells, for example ensuring that they are safe to use.

Legislation also impacts the way a business produces a product, through employment and health and safety laws. These can have huge cost implications.

Economic situation

The economic situation outside the control of a business can impact its operations. For example, a change in exchange rates could positively or negatively impact a business that imports products from overseas or that receives overseas incomes.

Environmental expectations

Consumers are becoming increasingly concerned with their environmental impact and as such, businesses need to be aware of this. They must examine their impact on the environment when manufacturing, packaging, transporting and selling products, as more and more customers are making purchasing decisions based on this factor.

Explain **two** economic changes that can affect a business. [4]

One change could be a reduction in interest rates[1] which would lead to increased consumer spending.[1] Another change could be increased unemployment[1] which would make it easier to recruit new employees.[1] Inflation[1] may increase sharply, reducing demand and consumer spending on non-essential goods and services.[1]

Other potential economic changes include gross domestic product,[1] exchange rates,[1] taxes[1] and consumer spending.[1]

BUSINESS OWNERSHIP

When an entrepreneur decides to start up a business, they have a number of different options for its formation. Each option will have an impact on the legal status of the business.

Liability

Unlimited liability

If an entrepreneur has **unlimited liability**, then they and the business are seen as the same legal entity. This is known as being **unincorporated**. Any debts that the business has will be the total responsibility of the owner. If the business cannot pay the debts off, then the owner may have to sell personal possessions to clear them.

Limited liability

If an entrepreneur has **limited liability**, then they are seen as separate from the business in the eyes of the law. This is called **incorporation**. Therefore, the debts of the business are not regarded as personal debts of the owner, so their personal possessions are protected and there is a guaranteed limit to their losses. The entrepreneur is only liable for the amount of money that they have invested.

Sole trader

A **sole trader** is a type of business that is owned and operated by one person.

Benefits

- Quick and easy to set up.
- Sole trader keeps all the profits.
- Sole trader controls all the decisions.
- Business' financial information is kept private.

Drawbacks

- Sole trader faces unlimited liability.
- May be more difficult to raise finance.
- Business may not run if sole trader is off sick or takes holiday.
- Heavy workload.
- Need to possess a wide range of skills.

Partnership

A **partnership** is an unincorporated business which has two or more owners who share the risk.

Benefits

- Each partner could contribute finance.
- Each partner can bring ideas and different skills.
- The workload can be shared.
- Business' financial information is kept private.
- Control is shared between partners.

Drawbacks

- Partners face unlimited liability.
- There may be disagreements between the partners.
- Profits are shared amongst partners according to agreed ratios.

Agreements between partners

Partners draw up an agreement explaining how their partnership will work. It will include the following details:

- How **profits** are to be shared.
- The **salary** levels of the partners.
- The percentage **voting rights** of each partner.
- How the **workload** is to be shared.
- The level of **investment** by each partner.
- The **sharing of liability**.
- The **decision-making process** (and decision-making powers of each partner).

Shola wants to open a small hotel, in his local coastal village, that will appeal to holiday makers with an environmental conscience. His idea is to run a completely green hotel, using renewable energy to provide the power needed. He is also intending to only use food that he is growing in the grounds of the hotel, or local organic produce if he can't grow what he needs. The project is expensive and although Shola has some savings, he would need help to finance the project. He is worried about the high interest rates that the bank will charge. Originally, he had thought about running and owning the hotel on his own, but lately has been wondering whether his friend, Ash, would want to join him. Ash used to own two restaurants but recently sold them to a bigger chain.

Recommend whether Shola should seek a partnership with Ash for his hotel business. [9]

One reason that Shola should start up as a partnership is that to run the environmentally friendly hotel will be expensive.[✓] This is because he will need to purchase all the equipment so that he can provide a sufficient amount of renewable energy (e.g. solar panels etc).[✓] This is on top of purchasing the premises and all the equipment and furniture needed to run a successful hotel.[✓] Shola does not have sufficient funds to do this,[✓] but by entering a partnership with Ash he may well do.[✓] This is because Ash has finance from previous businesses that were sold.[✓] This will mean that Shola won't have to seek finance from the bank, which would carry high interest[✓] and therefore end up costing him more in the long term.[✓] However, whether Shola should take on a partner is very dependent on Ash's objectives.[✓] Shola has a very clear vision of how he wants this hotel to run. By partnering with Ash there may be disagreements as Ash may not want to run it purely as an environmentally friendly hotel.[✓] This is owing to it being more expensive to do so.[✓] Ash may want to keep costs low in order to get a return on investment more quickly,[✓] reducing the risk of exposure of start-up funds from the restaurant sale.[✓] If this is not the case and Ash is happy to wait longer term for a return on investment, then starting this eco-hotel as a partnership would be the right thing to do.[✓]

This question will be marked in accordance with the levels-based mark scheme on page 106.

COMPANIES

A company is a business that is owned by those that have invested in it; these are called **shareholders**. Shareholders have limited liability and receive dividends (a share of the profit), in return for their investment.

Private limited companies (ltd)

This is an incorporated business which is owned by shareholders. Shares can only be sold privately, with the permission of the other existing shareholders, usually to friends and family.

Benefits

- Easier to raise finance by selling shares.
- Owners have **limited liability**.
- Directors are often also shareholders and can benefit from dividend payments.

Drawbacks

- Overall control could be lost.
- The company's accounts and financial information is not private.
- More legal paperwork is involved when setting up as it is more complex.

Public limited companies (plc)

This is an incorporated business owned by shareholders. Anyone can buy shares in the business. PLCs can access huge financial resources by selling shares on a stock exchange. This is achieved through **flotation**. A public limited company is controlled and managed by a Board of Directors who are voted into the position by shareholders at an **Annual General Meeting (AGM)**.

Benefits

- Can raise large amounts of finance by selling new shares to the general public.
- Shareholders have **limited liability**.
- Public are more aware of the business and perceive them as more reliable.

Drawbacks

- At risk from potential takeovers.
- Potential loss of control, for original owners, after flotation.
- There will be increased media scrutiny into their activities.
- Financial accounts are available for public viewing.

P B Martin operates as a sole trader with two butcher's shops that have been successful due to the excellent quality of the meat and customer service that they provide. They are looking to expand by opening up further shops around their county and also hoping to start supplying meat to be sold in major supermarkets. Despite their success, they do not have enough profit to cover the cost of this ambitious expansion.

Analyse the benefits to P B Martin of converting from a sole trader to a private limited company. [6]

The expansion plans will be very expensive and require the business to purchase more premises to sell their meat from,[✓] and to invest in more animals/stock if sufficient meat is to be produced to supply the supermarkets.[✓] By becoming a private limited company, their friends and family will be able to invest in the butchery business[✓] because shares can be sold privately.[✓] This means that larger amounts of finance can be raised[✓] so that they can purchase the stock and shops needed.[✓] The business may also be able to borrow more as a limited company[✓] and would benefit from limited liability[✓] if they were ever unable to repay the loan. Compared with using their own profits, this will be more effective at raising the amount of finance needed, as despite their current success, they do not have sufficient profits to pay for this expansion.[✓]

This question will be marked in accordance with the levels-based mark scheme on page 105.

NOT-FOR-PROFIT ORGANISATIONS

Not-for-profit organisations exist in order to achieve social objectives by benefiting others in some way, rather than making a profit for those that own them.

Examples

Examples of not-for-profit organisations include social enterprises, youth clubs and charities, such as the National Trust, WWF and Cancer Research UK.

Not-for-profit organisations could be unincorporated or they may be a company (incorporated).

Benefits

- Reputational benefits from contributing to society in some way.
- Employees may be more committed to work for a business that does good for others.

Drawbacks

- May find it difficult to raise finance.
- Financial statements may be closely scrutinised by the general public.

Case Study: Born in the challenging backdrop of a West African village, Kwame weathered the storms of hardship from an early age as his country was in civil war. With dreams that transcended the limitations of his circumstances, he embarked on a journey that led him to the bustling streets of London as a refugee. Determined to break the cycle of adversity, Kwame drew upon his resilience and founded a not-for-profit children's youth club. Nestled in the heart of the city, the club became a sanctuary for boys and girls from disadvantaged backgrounds. Here, they found solace and inspiration through free sports, ecology and educational classes, transforming their struggles into opportunity.

Explain **one** reason why Kwame many have wanted to set up a not-for-profit business. [4]

Kwame wanted to set up his youth club to help children facing adversity.[✓] As a child he was a refugee as his country was experiencing civil war and he may not have wanted other children to have to face hardship like he did.[✓] Therefore, he set up his youth club to benefit the lives of children who probably could not afford to pay for the sport, ecology and educational classes that he provides.[✓] The wellbeing of the children will be more important than profit to Kwame.[✓]

This question will be marked in accordance with the levels-based mark scheme on page 105.

SETTING BUSINESS AIMS AND OBJECTIVES

An **aim** is what a business hopes to achieve in the long term. It can also be referred to as the goal of a business; it is the reason that the business is in existence. An **objective** is more specific and is the short-term target that a business seeks in order to fulfil their aim.

Aims and objectives

Survival: Businesses must bring in enough to cash to pay for all their bills so that they can continue to trade. Sufficient **cash flow** is crucial to survival.

Growth: A well-established business that is financially successful may decide to grow, either **domestically** or **internationally** by expanding operations overseas.

Customer satisfaction: A business may seek to improve their customer satisfaction rating. This is done by improving the level of customer service or by increasing the range of products available.

The objectives set will differ between businesses depending on the size of the business, level of competition faced and type of business, for example not-for-profit organisations.

Profit maximisation: Business revenue that exceeds its costs creates profit. This is the main objective for many businesses, particularly those in the private sector. This can be achieved by focusing on growth or on **lowering costs**.

Market share: This is the percentage of the total sales in a market made by one business. Sometimes a business will prioritise increasing their market share so that they can become the dominant firm.

Social and ethical objectives: A business may prioritise the people around them or decide to place moral values above maximising profit. It will try to do the right thing for society.

Shareholder value: Businesses will want to reward their owners. They can do this by giving them dividends from the business' profits. Another way is by achieving business success which causes the value of any shares to rise.

Explain **two** reasons why a business might set objectives. [4]

To provide a target,[1] therefore the business' performance by comparison can be judged and necessary action taken.[1] To provide direction / to motivate employees,[1] because they all understand the common goal they are working towards.[1]

Other reasons include: To make it clear what the business wants to achieve.[1] To focus resources on achieving the objective.[1]

CHANGING OBJECTIVES AND MEASURING SUCCESS

A business may change its objective for a variety of reasons. It may have **become more established**, it may have already **achieved the last objective** or there may be **changes in the external environment** (see **pages 24-33**.)

Changing objectives

As a business first starts out, it will want to survive, as many new enterprises quickly fail. As they become more established, businesses will want to grow in order to increases sales and profit.

Once one objective is achieved, a business will set itself a new objective. Once profit is achieved, a business may then seek to become dominant in the market or look to grow either domestically or overseas. Larger businesses that operate in many countries may then start to prioritise their impact on the environment, or try to benefit those around them by having more ethical and social objectives.

How to answer 4 mark 'Explain' questions that are not linked to a specific business but ask you to look at two reasons or factors.

These questions require you to make a valid point and then to give a linked strand of development. You would then need to do this twice. The response to the question opposite shows this. There are two reasons recognised (more established and the country going into a recession), both of which are supported by a linked strand of development.

Explain **two** reasons why the objectives of a business may change over time. [4]

A business may become more established.[1] Therefore they would look to increase sales rather than simply survive.[1] Changes in the external environment / economic situation, such as the country entering a recession[1] would mean that a business may have to focus on survival as sales would likely fall.[1]

Use of objectives in judging success

The most common way that objectives are used to judge business performance is through measuring the level of profit made. However, objectives can be set that help a business measure success in alternative ways, these include:

- Customer satisfaction.
- Shareholder value.
- Product quality.
- Reputation.
- Social and ethical objectives.

STAKEHOLDERS

A **stakeholder** is an individual or group that has an interest in the way that a business operates. Each stakeholder will have a different objective and can be affected in different ways by the decisions a business makes. The interests of each stakeholder group, often come into conflict with each other.

Objectives of stakeholders

Stakeholder	What they want from the business
Shareholder (Owner)	Shareholders will commonly want the business to be financially successful so they can maximise the profits or dividends that are made on their investment.
Employees	Workers will want job security and financial reward in return for their effort.
Customers	Customers will want the product or service to fulfil their needs. They will expect good customer service and value for money.
Suppliers	Suppliers will want the business to be successful, so they can continue to receive orders. They will also want to be paid on time.
Local community	Local residents will want the business to be successful, so it continues to offer employment. They will also want the business to do good for their community, both in terms of the environment and in terms of their provision.
Pressure groups	Pressure groups will want businesses to behave in an ethically and environmentally friendly manner. These can include trade unions who may campaign for workers' rights.
The Government	The Government will want businesses to be successful so that they continue to employ people. Businesses also pay tax to the government.

Impact and influence of stakeholders on businesses

The owners and managers of a business will have a controlling influence on its activity, but they cannot ignore the other stakeholders as they have an influence on how the business operates:

- A business cannot ignore its customers. If they are not listened to, they will purchase products from rivals instead.
- A business needs a happy and motivated workforce so must consider their needs.
- Not paying attention to the needs of suppliers can lead to poor relationships with them.
- Ignoring the wishes of the local community and pressure groups could cause the business to develop a negative reputation.

Explain **one** possible conflict between stakeholders that a business may experience. [2]

Conflict may exist between owners, who want to make as much profit as possible, and employees, who want to receive higher pay.[1] *They may be in conflict as both cannot happen - if employees' pay is increased then costs will also increase, sacrificing profit.*[1]

BUSINESS LOCATION

The location that a business chooses can have a huge impact on its success. There are various factors that will determine which location is best. These vary in importance depending on the nature of the business.

Factors influencing the location decision of a business

Competition: Some businesses will choose to locate far away from their competitors so that they are the only supplier of a good or service in that area. Others may choose to locate close to their rivals as this is where customers are likely to be, for example, a shopping mall.

Availability of raw materials: Some businesses may require large bulky raw materials, such as timber, to be able to produce their product. Transporting the supplies to the business may be expensive so, to keep costs down, businesses may choose to locate close to the raw materials they need.

Costs: Not all businesses can afford to locate wherever they want. The cost of the most sought-after locations will be more expensive. Therefore, a business on a budget may choose a location based on cost.

Labour: Businesses need sufficient available workers close by who have the required skills. A business needs to locate close to where people are willing and able to work.

Proximity to market: For some businesses, being close to their customers will be the most important factor. By doing this, it can raise awareness of the business and help it to become established. This is particularly important for retail businesses.

Nature of the business activity

The most important factors mentioned above, depend on the nature of the activity that a business is involved in. A manufacturing firm may need to be close to supplies, while a service sector business will need to be close to customers.

Which **one** of the following is a reason why a business may decide to locate overseas? [1]

A – A business will pay higher tax in the country they are located in.

B – It will be easier to transport the goods back to the UK.

C – Language and cultural barriers may improve trading.

D – The cost of labour may be cheaper.

D. The cost of labour may be cheaper.[1]

BUSINESS PLANNING

A **business plan** is a working document that details the objectives that a business wants to achieve and how it will set about achieving them. It looks at all aspects of the business so that risk is reduced, giving the business a greater chance to succeed.

Purpose of business planning

There are many reasons why a business would create a business plan. Although it does not guarantee success it will be advantageous in the following ways.

To plan for the setting up of a business: Through planning, an entrepreneur should be able to think ahead and assess the risks that they may face, allowing them to make better informed decisions.

To detail how functions of a business will be organised: Through business planning, an entrepreneur can ensure each functional area (marketing, operations, HR and finance) is sufficiently resourced and considered.

To predict future problems: Producing a business plan cannot guarantee that a business will be successful. There will always be the risk that something unforeseen could happen which could negatively impact on the business. However, by producing a business plan, an entrepreneur will be thinking about a lot of different potential scenarios and how the business could deal with them.

To raise finance: Any potential investor will want to know that their investment is as secure as possible. Although risk cannot be eliminated, a business plan can show potential investors what income and costs have been considered.

To motivate employees: Business planning helps all those connected with a business to understand its purpose and how their role within the business can help to achieve these objectives. This can be motivating.

Setting objectives: A business plan will detail what the business hopes to achieve. By monitoring progress against these objectives, entrepreneurs can make appropriate decisions to help achieve success.

You will not be expected to write a business plan.

Drawbacks of business planning

- The usefulness of the business plan is dependent on the experience and knowledge of the entrepreneur.
- Not all risk is removed. Although planning helps reduce the level of risk faced, market conditions and external factors change, so business success is not guaranteed.

SECTIONS OF A BUSINESS PLAN

A business plan needs to consider all aspects of a business, including some background information on the entrepreneur and details of their idea. Each of the functions will also be considered.

Example

Details of the entrepreneur:
- Experience and skills of the entrepreneur(s).

Financial forecasts:
- Budgets of revenue and expenditure.
- Cash-flow forecasts.
- Breakeven analysis.

Marketing:
- Market research to be carried out.
- Details of the target market.
- Details of the marketing mix.
- Details of the competitors and how a business will compete.

Business name

PROPOSAL

MARKET ANALYSIS

The business idea:
- Details of proposed business activity.
- The business' aims and objectives.
- The legal structure of the business.
- How the business is to be financed.

Resources required:
- Details of supplies needed and the suppliers the business will use.
- The equipment and machinery that is necessary.

Staff required:
- The number of employees needed and the skill sets that they must possess.
- How the business is to be structured including job roles and pay structures.

BASIC FINANCIAL CALCULATIONS

To be able to accurately calculate **profit**, a business will need to know its **revenue** and its **total costs**.

Revenue

Revenue is also referred to as **sales revenue** or **turnover**. It is the total amount of income made from selling a product or service. It is calculated by using the following formula:

Revenue = selling price × number of units sold

Fixed and variable costs

Fixed costs are those that do not change in line with changes in output. Examples include **advertising**, **rent**, **insurance**, **salaries**, **finance payments** and **rates**.

Variable costs are those that will change directly with changes in output. An example would be **raw materials**. The formula for total variable costs is:

Total variable costs = variable cost per unit × number of units sold

Utility bills, such as electricity or telephone bills, could be either fixed or variable so it is best to avoid this answer unless you can clarify your response.

Total costs

Total costs are all the costs added together in making a product or providing a service.

Total costs = fixed costs + variable costs

Profit and loss

Profit is made when the revenue received exceeds the total costs. If a business has total costs that are greater than revenue it is called a **loss**.

Profit = Revenue − total costs

Frank has a business plan for a mobile hairdressing service. He is expecting to have 75 customers in his first month, charging them £20 each. He has provided you with the following cost information for his first month of trading:

- cost of materials needed for each haircut: £3.50
- average cost of travel to each customer: £1.50
- fixed costs: £450

(a) Calculate Frank's profit for his first month of trading. [5]

(b) Identify **two** fixed costs for Frank's business. [2]

(a) Variable cost per haircut = 3.50 + 1.50 = £5[1]

Total variable costs = £5 × 75 customers = £375[1]

Total costs = £450 + £375 = £825[1]

Revenue = £20 × 75 = £1,500[1]

Profit = £1,500 − £825 = £675[1]

(b) Two from: Rent,[1] insurance,[1] salaries,[1] advertising,[1] loan interest payments,[1] rates.[1]

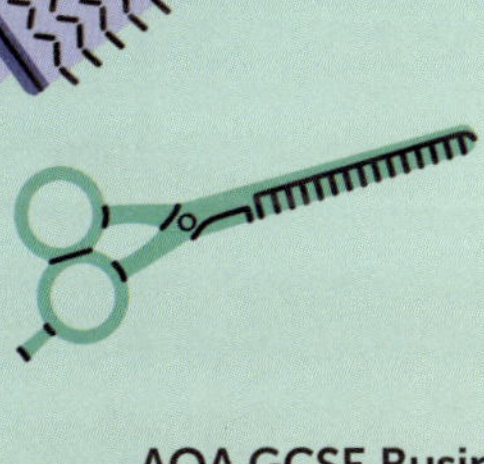

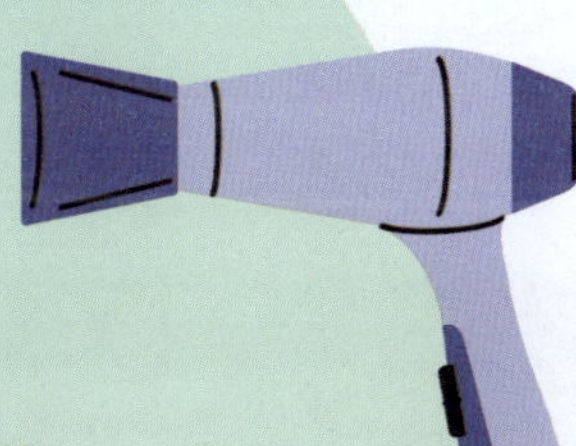

EXPANDING A BUSINESS

After surviving the initial years and becoming established, a business may want to grow. The owners will have to make a decision as to whether to grow organically (internally) or externally.

Organic growth

Organic growth is characterised by a business that grows by increasing its output, by increasing its customer base or by developing new products. It is also called **internal growth**. Methods of organic growth are:

Franchising

A central business (**franchisor**) licenses other entrepreneurs (**franchisees**) giving them rights to sell the products of the business, usually in return for a fee and a percentage of revenue or profits.

Benefits

- A lot of the risk of running a business is taken on by the franchisee.
- The business will receive **royalties** and also a potential lump sum.
- It is a quick way to achieve growth.

Drawbacks

- The actions of one franchisee can impact the entire brand and business' reputation.
- Franchisees take a large amount of the profits.
- There is some loss of control.

Opening new stores

A business can keep control and decide to reach more customers by opening new stores in different locations, or if it's in the secondary sector, by opening more factories. This method can be expensive as the business will have to provide the finance.

E-commerce

E-commerce involves the buying and selling of products online. By locating online, the business can target an entirely new market, potentially from anywhere in the world, who can purchase at any time of day. They may also reduce the need for expensive retail store rental. However, for businesses selling tangible products, it can be expensive to distribute its goods and they could see a fall in their sales in stores.

Outsourcing

Outsourcing means contracting another business to produce your own products for you. A business may choose to expand in this way as they may not have the financial capability to increase its production facilities to the required level, helping to keep costs low, while growing rapidly. However, the business is dependent on the contractor. If the business they buy from experiences quality issues, it can harm their reputation.

External growth happens when a business grows by joining with another business, whether that be by a merger or a takeover. It is also known as **inorganic growth**.

Mergers and takeovers

A **merger** is where two or more businesses agree to join to share resources. A **takeover** is where one business buys a majority shareholding in another.

Benefits	Drawbacks
• Growth can be quicker than internal growth. • Combined businesses benefit from shared resources and skills.	• Difficult to integrate two businesses together. • It can be an expensive process.

Adam runs a manufacturing firm, The Sugar Fix Ltd, producing handmade luxury desserts, that he sells in retail outlets around Northumberland. Adam has built up a reputation of quality for his desserts, which has resulted in high demand, despite the high prices he charges. He is now looking to expand and is considering an offer to merge with a rival firm called The Sweet Spot, which produce a budget range of desserts, but have a wider distribution, selling their products in supermarkets around the north of England.

Explain **one** reason why Adam would want to merge The Sugar Fix with rivals, The Sweet Spot. [4]

Merging the two businesses together will allow them to share resources.[✔] For Adam, this will mean that he will have access to the supermarkets as a distribution channel, which he wouldn't have had without the merger.[✔] This will mean that he would have an opportunity to sell the premium desserts to the supermarkets as well, so is likely to sell more desserts.[✔] This is because more people shop at supermarkets and will see his luxury range.[✔] As a result Adam will have a greater share of the dessert market.[✔]

BENEFITS OF EXPANDING A BUSINESS

Economies of scale

Economies of scale is the cost advantage of producing on a large scale. As output increases, the unit cost decreases. This allows products to be sold at a cheaper price, or the business can choose to keep prices the same and earn more profit per product sold. There are two different types of economies of scale:

Purchasing economies of scale

This means a business can order materials in bulk from a supplier and receive a discounted price, thereby reducing units costs.

Technical economies of scale

Enables a larger business to take advantage of advancements in technology to obtain bigger and better equipment and machinery. In turn, this allows them to produce products at a lower cost per unit.

Calculating average unit per cost

To calculate the **average cost per unit**, you need to use the following formula:

Average unit cost = total costs ÷ number of units produced

For example, look at the table below:

Units produced	Total cost	Average unit cost
1000	£250,000	£250 (250,000 ÷ 1000)
2000	£400,000	£200 (400,000 ÷ 2000)
3000	£510,000	£170 (510,000 ÷ 3000)
4000	£600,000	£150 (600,000 ÷ 4000)

The table shows the effects that economies of scale have on the average unit cost of production. It is cheaper, per unit, to produce 4000 than it is to produce 1000.

Promotional benefits

Larger firms can often spend more money on advertising which helps them to become more well known. If the business is more well known, it increases the chances of success for any new product launched as people are more likely to trust a known brand.

Workforce benefits

Successful growth will lead to more people in the industry becoming aware of a business. As a result, more people will want to be involved through employment, so the managers will have a greater pool of potential recruits. This will mean that it is more likely that the business will recruit people with the skills (and they need.

DRAWBACKS OF EXPANDING A BUSINESS

Drawbacks of expansion

Expanding a business does not guarantee that it will become more successful. There are some dangers that come with increased size. These include:

Communication

Larger businesses often suffer from **poorer communication**. This is because there will be a lot more people employed so communication between workers in different sections is less efficient. This can lead to mistakes being made.

Coordination

There could be **coordination issues** with a larger workforce. This means that not all workers may be working towards the same goal.

Motivation

With a larger workforce, there is greater risk that some workers become isolated and therefore suffer **reduced motivation** as they may not feel valued or part of the team.

Management

As businesses become larger, they may suffer from **management issues**. Having a larger workforce makes it more challenging to manage and support every employee.

These issues can lead to **diseconomies of scale**.

Explain **one** impact on a business from experiencing diseconomies of scale. [2]

One impact is that the average cost of production rises as workers become less productive.[1] This is because they may not feel so valued by the business.[1]

Landmark Motors plc is a UK based car manufacturing business with operations nationwide. Their biggest selling car, the Landmark Boost, is a small, competitively priced hatchback. (Table 1 below shows some financial information for the car.) One of the reasons they can offer low prices is that the business has been able to keep costs low. As they have grown, they have benefitted from introducing the latest technology, that has made the production lines more efficient, producing cars in 20% less time than when they first started out.

Having been established since 1956, Landmark has steadily grown into a market leader in the UK. Over the past 5 years, sales have remained at a constant level, but the directors of the company are wanting to grow the company by selling more cars overseas, particularly in China. To achieve this objective, the directors know that they will have to increase production of their cars and are considering taking over a rival Chinese car manufacturer in order to do this, particularly as labour costs are much lower there than they are in the UK. However, some of the board members are concerned that this poses too much of a risk and that they should grow by opening up new manufacturing plants in the UK.

	£
Selling price	£9,995
Variable cost per car	£2,500
Monthly fixed costs	£3,750,000

Table 1 – Financial information relating to the Landmark Boost

EXAMINATION PRACTICE

1. Which **one** of the following is a method of external growth? [1]
    A – E-commerce
    B – Merger
    C – Opening new stores
    D – Outsourcing

2. Which sector of business activity involves providing a service for a customer? [1]
    A – Manufacturing
    B – Primary
    C – Secondary
    D - Tertiary

3. Identify **two** variable costs. [2]

4. Explain **one** impact that environmental expectations could have on a business. [2]

5. Explain **one** reason why a business would create a business plan. [2]

6. Explain **one** way a business can use objectives to measure success. [2]

7. Explain **one** way in which a stakeholder may impact on a business. [2]

For the following questions, you must refer to Case study 1 on the previous page.

8. Identify **two** different stakeholders that will be impacted by the takeover of the Chinese car
    manufacturer. [2]

9. Landmark plan to sell 5,000 cars a month.
    Using the information in **Table 1**, calculate the profit that they would make. [4]

10. Explain **one** type of economy of scale that Landmark might benefit from. [4]

11. Analyse the drawbacks to Landmark of being a public limited company. [6]

12 Analyse the factors that may impact where Landmark chooses to locate. [6]

13. Recommend whether Landmark should grow through a takeover. [9]

TECHNOLOGY

As technology advances, it presents businesses with many opportunities in terms of innovating products and production processes. However, those business that do not embrace technology or are slow to develop with it, can very quickly become uncompetitive.

How technology influences business activity

Advancements in technology has an impact on all functional areas of business activity:

Business operations

Technology has enabled businesses to be more efficient in their production processes and has enabled many firms to locate online, dispensing with the need for expensive physical premises.

Human resources

As technology has enabled automation of the production process, many businesses have saved costs by needing fewer manual labourers, reducing wages. Technology has also changed the way that people work, with many jobs now being able to be done at home.

Marketing

Technology has changed the way in which businesses communicate with their customers. The use of social media and digital communications means more expensive, traditional forms of communication are not required. Businesses can utilise technology to gain information on customers, i.e. loyalty cards inform a business about customers' buying habits.

Finance

Although technology usually comes with an initial cost, long term savings can be made where technology reduces other costs in all functional areas. For example, technological advancements have meant that businesses can now use electronic cashless payment systems to transfer money quickly and safely, allowing more convenient and seamless purchase of its products for consumers.

Explain **one** drawback that advancements in technology might have on a business. [2]

A business may need to invest heavily at the start which can be very expensive.[1]
This means that in the short-term, costs could increase.[1]

E-commerce

E-commerce is the buying and selling of goods and services by electronic transaction over the Internet. It allows customers to make purchases at any time of day and at their own convenience. **M-commerce** is the use of mobile devices to buy and sell products online. See **page 79**.

Benefits of e-commerce

- Allows access to wider markets as consumers from anywhere in the world can purchase products from the business via a website.
- E-commerce businesses may no longer need expensive physical retail locations so costs can be saved.
- E-commerce has helped businesses (especially new ones) to grow quickly and organically.

Digital communication

Digital communication (**information and communications technology**) involves contacting customers electronically. This has changed the way that businesses communicate with stakeholders.

You are expected to know relevant examples of digital communication.

ETHICAL AND ENVIRONMENTAL CONSIDERATIONS

As society becomes more aware of ethical and environmental issues, there is growing pressure on businesses to behave responsibly. Although this brings many benefits, it involves a trade-off with profit that may have a negative impact on financial performance.

Ethical considerations

Ethics provide a guiding principle that shapes the character of a business. There is often a trade-off between profit and being ethically responsible.

- A business may choose to pay workers a fair wage rather than exploiting them.
- A business may choose to improve the working facilities and conditions of employees.
- A business may choose to pay suppliers a fair amount for their materials.
- A business may choose to source resources ethically.
- A business may choose to be honest and treat customers fairly.
- A business may choose to be fair to local residents, often investing in community projects to ensure they have a positive impact on society.

Benefits of acting ethically

- Reputational benefits.
- Can be a unique selling point (USP).
- Can be motivating for employees.
- May help to attract more talented workers.

Drawbacks of acting ethically

- More expensive to source raw materials.
- Training workers to be ethical can be expensive.
- Providing better staff facilities can increase costs.
- May have to charge a higher price, losing trade to lower priced, less ethical businesses.

Explain the trade off between behaving ethically and profit. [2]

Behaving ethically, such as paying your workers a fair wage for their work, will increase costs.[1] As a result, the business will not make as much profit as it possibly could have done.[1]

Through its activities, a business has the potential to impact the environment, in the following ways:

Traffic congestion

Businesses will receive deliveries; employees will need to travel to their place of work and customers may visit the business as well. This all adds to the traffic on already busy roads.

Waste disposal

Manufacturing firms in particular, are likely to create a lot of waste that needs disposing of. Disposing of this waste can be damaging for the environment and local wildlife.

Noise and air pollution

Some businesses, such as airports, will significantly add to noise pollution in a local area, while other businesses may contribute to poorer air quality either through emitting gases in the production process or simply through generating an increased amount of traffic on the roads.

Recycling

Businesses can lessen their impact on the environment by recycling waste and producing products that can be repaired or recycled. This limits the amount that is dumped in landfill sites.

Sustainability

Sustainable production is production that can continue long term and doesn't have a harmful impact on the environment. This can be achieved through:

- Investing in **renewable energy** and using electric vehicles to distribute products.
- Using locally sourced materials rather than purchasing from afar, thus reducing **product miles** and **carbon footprint**.
- Using biodegradable packaging rather than single-use plastics.
- Recycling waste, and making products from recycled or renewable materials.
- Cleaning up all waste rather than dumping it.
- Producing products without use of chemicals or other harmful ingredients.

Global warming

Businesses are increasingly conscious about their impact on global warming. However, reducing emissions, using renewal energy sources and lowering their carbon footprint can all increase costs, lowering profit.

Scarce resources

Non-renewable fuels such as coal and oil are commonly cheaper for companies to use than green energy sources despite their increasing scarcity and damaging carbon output.

THE ECONOMIC CLIMATE ON BUSINESS

As society becomes more aware of ethical and environmental issues, there is growing pressure on businesses to behave responsibly. Although this brings many benefits, it involves a trade-off with profit that may have a negative impact on financial performance.

Interest rates

Interest rates are the rates charged for borrowing money over a period of time, or the reward for saving money. This applies to loans, overdrafts, mortgages and savings.

Increase in interest rates

This will increase the cost of borrowing to both businesses and consumers and will have the following impacts:

- Businesses who have taken out loans may see an increase in costs.
- Businesses are less likely to borrow money as it is now more expensive to do so.
- Consumers will have less disposable income as they have to repay more on any borrowed money or may be more inclined to save money with more favourable rates.

Decrease in interest rates

The cost of borrowing is reduced and will have the following impacts:

- Business costs will decrease for those that have borrowed money.
- More businesses will be encouraged to borrow and spend money as it may be cheaper to do so.
- Consumers will be more inclined to spend money as borrowing money from banks or spending on credit cards will be cheaper.

You do not need to understand economic theory as to why interest rates change, just that they do and how the changes impact businesses.

Level of employment

Unemployment exists in an economy when there are people of working age who want to work but cannot find a job. High levels of unemployment can be negative for a business because:

- Many consumers will have less disposable income.
- The level of demand in an economy will fall.
- Sales levels will decrease.
- As demand and sales fall, businesses may need fewer workers, so unemployment rises further.

Explain **one** benefit of high unemployment in an economy to a business. [2]

There will be many people who do not have a job,[1] therefore a business will have a greater pool of potential candidates to select from when recruiting.[1]

A business may experience lower labour turnover,[1] because there are fewer jobs available for employees to leave for.[1]

There will be lots of skilled people out of work,[1] therefore a business can employ people on reduced / more competitive wage rates.[1]

Consumer spending

Consumer spending (also known as disposable income) is the amount of money that consumers have left to spend after they have paid for all their living expenses and bills. Economic variables affect the level of **disposable income** through:

- Changes in the level of inflation.
- Changes in the level of unemployment.
- Changes in the interest rate.
- Changes in taxation.
- The economy entering a recession.

Income levels in an economy will have a significant impact on the level of **demand**. If consumers have more disposable income, then the level of demand will increase. This will lead to a business' sales level increasing.

GLOBALISATION

Globalisation is the expansion of trade by businesses to operate internationally across many different countries. It is having an increasing impact on how businesses operate as more compete internationally.

How UK businesses compete internationally

Better designs

Product design includes the functionality, appearance and features of a product. A product that is well designed will help a business to better meet customer needs, therefore they are more likely to purchase the product and increase loyalty as they become attached to the brand.

Higher quality products at lower prices

A higher quality product is one that better satisfies its customers. When competing internationally, if a business can produce a product that is deemed to be value for money, by being of a higher perceived quality, but priced at a level equal to, or below, products of inferior quality, then a business is more likely to be successful.

Benefits and drawbacks of globalisation

+ Rapid growth

Businesses can experience a large increase in sales in a short period of time by selling their products in new overseas markets.

+ Cheaper resources

Businesses that use materials in their production process can now potentially get cheaper resources from a broader range of overseas suppliers.

+ Inward investment

Inward investment refers to organisations or individuals from overseas that invest capital into UK businesses and industries. This has allowed them to grow and infrastructure to be improved.

Explain **one** drawback to UK businesses from increased levels of globalisation. [2]

Increased competition[1] from foreign sellers that may be able to manufacture their goods at a lower cost and therefore sell them at a lower price / easier for foreign businesses to start selling their product in the UK.[1]

Increased risk of takeover,[1] because it's now easier for overseas businesses to buy UK companies.[1]

Exchange rates

An **exchange rate** is the price of one currency in terms of another. Whether a change in the exchange rate impacts positively on a business will be dependent on whether the pound is strengthening or weakening, and whether the business exports or imports goods.

You will not be required to calculate exchange rate conversions, but you do need to understand the impact of a change in exchange rates on a UK business' sales and profits.

Imports and exports

Imports

Imports are the goods and services bought from a supplier in another country. The rise of globalisation has meant that consumers can more easily buy goods from foreign companies. This means that UK firms will face more competition, making it harder to survive. Although, those that import raw materials now have a greater opportunity to source these more cheaply abroad.

Exports

Exports are the goods and services produced in one country and sold to another. The rise of globalisation has opened up new markets overseas for UK businesses to sell their products to. This has given businesses opportunities to grow and potentially increase their profits.

Impact of changing exchange rates on UK businesses

↑ Impact of an increase in value of the pound

- Cheaper to import materials from abroad in £s.
- Poor for exporters as the price of exports will rise for international customers.
- Domestic businesses suffer as customers buy cheaper products from abroad.

↓ Impact of a decrease in value of the pound

- Costs more to import materials from abroad in £s.
- Good for exporters as the price of exports, in terms of foreign currencies, falls.
- Good news for domestic businesses as imports become more expensive.

LEGISLATION

There are various pieces of legislation that state how businesses must behave. Employment law governs how businesses interact and deal with their workers. Health and safety laws are there to protect employees from coming to harm whilst at work. Consumer law ensures that buyers are protected from being exploited by businesses.

Employment law

Employment legislation is enforced in order to protect workers. Various laws are in place to stop employees from being exploited by their employers. It covers the following areas:

Recruitment

Businesses must ensure that employees have a legal right to work in the UK. This involves completing checks on new employees.

Pay

All employees are entitled to receive a minimum wage. Workers aged over 25 years old and above are entitled to receive the **National Living Wage**, which is slightly more than the **National Minimum Wage**.

Discrimination

The Equality Act (2010) states that a business must not be discriminatory against employees. This includes discriminating because of age, gender, race, religion, sexual orientation or because of disability. The business must ensure that they pay people the same amount of money for the same work completed.

1. Explain **one** impact on a business from not complying with employment law. [2]

   If a business pays its workers below the National Minimum Wage they are likely to be fined / taken to court by the employee / lose that member of staff,[1] which will decrease the business' profits / reflect poorly on their reputation / incur costs of retraining and recruitment of a replacement staff member.[1]

The national living and minimum wages are a minimum hourly rate set by the government. Any increases in these can significantly affect the labour costs for businesses who rely on low paid workers.

Health and safety law

All workers have the right to be kept safe whilst at work. The legislation that covers this is **The Health and Safety at Work Act** (1974). A business can ensure the safety of employees by:
- Providing training, protective equipment and clothing.
- Installing and maintaining safety equipment.
- Producing risk assessments of workspaces to ensure risks are controlled and minimised.
- Carrying out safety inspections.
- Ensuring employees have sufficient breaks.
- Displaying safety notices and instructions.

Consumer law

Consumer law is enforced to ensure that consumers are protected from malpractice by businesses. The law also includes trade descriptions which ensures that goods and services are accurately labelled and described. **The Consumer Rights Act** (2015) protects consumers by addressing the quality of products and the rights of the consumer by stating that:

Food products must be accurately labelled and described, clearly stating the ingredients. Electrical products must undergo testing to ensure that they are safe to use.

- Products should work properly and be fit for purpose.
- Products must be safe to use (or consume) and be of satisfactory quality.
- Products must be as described.
- Consumers have the right to return unsuitable products within a period of 30 days.
- A business is responsible for their goods until the customer has taken possession of them.
- A business must repair or replace faulty products or refund the customer.

The effect of legislation on businesses

Complying with consumer, employment and health and safety legislation can significantly increase the administration costs of a business in ensuring that everything is followed correctly. A business may also need to employ people specifically to ensure that the laws are followed and adhered to. However, the laws are also there to help businesses.

The advantages of legislation for businesses include:

- If a business is compliant with the law, then it cannot be fined, which saves the business from unnecessary or unplanned expense.
- By complying with consumer legislation, a business will gain a positive reputation which will help future sales.
- By doing the right thing by customers, a business can build better relationships, potentially leading to increased customer loyalty.
- Employees who will feel happier and better protected may be more motivated and therefore more productive.
- A business will be seen as a good employer and as such, will likely find it easier to recruit the people they need as well as retaining the staff they already have.

2. Identify and explain **two** ways that legislation may decrease the profits of a business. [4]

Health and safety legislation means that workers may have to be trained in the use of safety equipment.[1] Training will increase the costs of the business which may reduce profits.[1]

Businesses have to ensure that their products are safe for consumers to use.[1] This may incur additional expenditure in the production process, which reduces profits.[1]

COMPETITIVE ENVIRONMENT

A **market** is a place where buyers and sellers meet, and an exchange occurs. **Competition** exists when there is more than one business selling a similar product, each trying to attract the same customers.

Impact on businesses of operating in competitive markets

A business competes in a competitive market when it faces many rival businesses that are selling similar products to the same group of customers. This type of market can impact a business in the following areas:

Price

There will be pressure on businesses to lower prices so that they can attract more customers. This relies on being able to produce the product cost effectively, so enough profit is made on each sale. It also means that a business must sell a larger quantity to make a large overall profit.

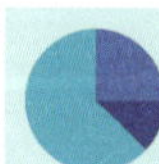

Market share

Market share is likely to be lower in competitive markets, for the simple fact that the customers have a greater number of businesses / similar products to choose from.

Innovation

In a market with lots of businesses selling similar products, there is pressure to create new and innovative products. A business that comes out with something unique is likely to attract customers away from rivals.

Explain **two** impacts on a business from operating in a market with little competition. [4]

One impact is that a business may be able to charge a higher price.[1] This is because there are not many, if any, other businesses selling similar products, therefore customers will have little other option than to pay the advertised price to buy the product.[1]

UNCERTAINTY AND RISKS

Uncertainty exists when the outcome of a particular course of action is unknown. **Risk** is the chance that something may go wrong. Businesses need to understand the risks that they face and take action to minimise them.

Risks faced by businesses

Businesses face constant uncertainty and risk which creates a degree of financial insecurity. Risk is often down to changes in the economic climate (see **page 28**) or in legislation (**page 32**). Other risks include:

Bad publicity: A customer may leave a negative review after a poor experience, which may negatively impact other people's perception of the business. This could also happen through negative media attention.

Not attracting enough customers: A business may experience a sudden fall in demand or may not make enough sales to cover their expenditure. This could be down to competition, overpricing or seasonal sales.

Increased competition: More businesses may enter the market and steal away a business' customers.

Loss of employees: A business could lose its key employees and not be able to replace them, causing a fall in productivity or the level of service provided.

Loss of resources: A business may lose their source of key materials. This may mean that they have to get materials from elsewhere, likely impacting costs or a product's overall quality.

Identify and explain **two** ways that an entrepreneur can minimise risk. [4]

One way is to create a business plan.[1] This will help an entrepreneur plan for all eventualities and what action they would take if an event occurred.[1]

They could carry out market research amongst their target market / of competitor behaviour or products,[1] which would help them identify the market needs / demand needs so they produce a product that customers want / understand the competition better to more effectively match and improve on quality.[1]

Other answers could include: training employees,[1] selling in different markets,[1] and a risk analysis of the threats to a business and its weaknesses.[1]

Reasons for starting a business

Despite the risks involved, many entrepreneurs still choose to start a business. The reasons for this include:

- To pursue an interest or hobby.
- To be their own boss.
- To earn profit.
- Because they are unhappy in their previous employment.

As a national fast-food chain, Wrap Nation has rapidly expanded its footprint by venturing into 20 countries worldwide, captivating taste buds with its signature filled burritos and wraps. Embracing the ethos of customisation, Wrap Nation empowers customers to tailor their meals, selecting from an array of fillings and accompaniments to suit their preferences. Enhancing the dining experience further, Wrap Nation introduced a user-friendly app, enabling patrons to pre-order their meals and have them ready upon arrival, saving time and improving convenience over their rivals, Bite.

However, amidst its global success, Wrap Nation faced scrutiny in a recent article which highlighted the excessive use of plastic in wrapping. The article showcased just how much wrapping was being discarded and thrown in landfill sites. It also highlighted the dangers of plastic packaging on the environment and eco-systems where it had been dumped.

To finance its ambitious expansion overseas, Wrap Nation turned to borrowing substantial sums of money from financial institutions. The Finance Director recently spoke about how she was worried about future profitability should UK interest rates increase dramatically as they are heavily financed by debt, including large bank loans.

The UK restaurants source many ingredients from European countries. These ingredients are of a much higher quality but Wrap Nation's reliance on these imports adds complexity to its supply chain management, not only in terms of delivery but also it leaves them susceptible to changes in the exchange rate between the Pound and the Euro.

EXAMINATION PRACTICE

1. Which **one** of the following is a drawback of using e-commerce?   [1]
    A – Allows access to wider markets.
    B – Expensive physical locations may no longer be required.
    C – Increased convenience for consumers.
    D – May not get noticed online amongst higher competition.

2. Which **one** of the following is true when an economy is experiencing high unemployment?   [1]
    A – Businesses will have a greater pool of potential candidates to recruit from.
    B – Consumer spending increases.
    C – Consumers will have more disposable income.
    D – Demand in an economy will rise.

3. Explain **one** way in which a business might communicate with customers digitally.   [2]

4. Explain **one** way in which a business' production could become more sustainable.   [2]

5. Explain **one** benefit to a business of globalisation.   [2]

6. Explain **one** risk faced by a business.   [2]

7. Identify and explain **two** ways that legislation might impact on a business.   [4]

For the following questions, you must refer to Case study 2 on the previous page.

8. Explain **one** impact on Wrap Nation from operating in a competitive market.   [4]

9. Explain **one** impact on Wrap Nation of the Pound increasing in value.   [4]

10. Analyse the benefits to Wrap Nation of technological advancements.   [6]

11. Analyse the impacts on Wrap Nation of an increase in interest rates.   [6]

12. Recommend whether Wrap Nation should change its packaging.   [9]

PRODUCTION PROCESSES

It is the purpose of the operations function within a business to produce goods and provide services to the customers. Products can be produced in a variety of ways and a business must choose which method is most suitable for them.

Methods of production

Job production

Job production involves the manufacture of a single, unique product to meet an individual order. An example of this would be the construction of a sports stadium or the making of a bespoke wedding dress.

Benefits

- Product meets the exact requirements of the customer.
- Product is unique, creating a USP.
- Motivating for staff as it involves skilled work.
- High profit margins, as high prices can be charged.

Drawbacks

- High unit costs, so a high price is set.
- A skilled workforce is required.
- Employees may require more training.
- Can take a longer time to produce, so productivity is low compared with flow.

Flow production

Flow production (also known as mass production) involves the assembly of goods along a production line, often using robotics. Products will be identical and manufactured continuously in large quantities. Examples include the production of chocolate bars and glass bottles.

Benefits

- Low average unit costs, because of economies of scale.
- High volumes of output are produced which can be increased to meet further demand.
- Use of robotics allows for 24/7 manufacture.
- **Specialisation** (where employees focus on a certain aspect of production) can occur, which boosts efficiency.

Drawbacks

- Expensive to set up due to the cost of machinery.
- Repetitive work is demotivating for employees.
- A breakdown on the production line halts all production.
- Business cannot adapt product easily, therefore lacks flexibility.
- Risk that equipment is not fully utilised, leaving spare capacity.

Efficiency is concerned with how well a business is using the resources it has in order to produce goods or provide services. A business becomes more efficient when it produces more goods or services with fewer inputs. Efficiency strategies include **lean production** and **just in time** (**JIT**).

1. Explain **one** benefit to a business of becoming more efficient. [2]

    One benefit is that the business will have lower unit costs[1] therefore the business can lower its price attracting more potential customers.[1]

Lean production

A **lean production** strategy aims to reduce the resources used to create products such as raw materials, labour, machines and premises. Waste can be in the form of unsold products, unused materials in the production process or workers' time that is not fully utilised. Having a lot of waste can be costly for a business, so by minimising it, a business can keep costs low and become more efficient.

Just in time (JIT)

Just in time stock control is used by businesses that hold no stock. Raw materials are ordered as they are needed and are used straight away on the production line once they arrive. (JIT is looked at in more detail on **page 40**.)

2. Identify and explain **two** ways in which JIT can help to make a business more efficient. [4]

    Using JIT means that the business holds no stock,[1] this minimises the risk to the business of having a lot of unsold stock going to waste / chance of theft / damage to stock.[1]

    Holding no stock means that a business does not have to pay for expensive storage units / manage warehousing,[1] therefore costs are kept to a minimum, boosting efficiency.[1]

MANAGING STOCK

Managing stock involves organising the raw materials that are used in production, work-in-progress and finished goods that are waiting to be sold. There are two main methods, **just in time (JIT)** and **just in case (JIC)**. A business must decide what is the most efficient method of controlling stock.

Just in time (JIT)

JIT organises procurement to ensure that the production process never runs out of stock, reducing the number of sales lost due to insufficient raw materials (see **page 39**). For this system to work, the business must have a good relationship with its supplier, as well as a well organised production system so it knows precisely when and what to order.

Benefits

- Reduced cost of holding stock.
- Don't need as much space to store stock.
- Reduced risk that stock gets damaged, becomes obsolete or is stolen.

Drawbacks

- Need to have more frequent deliveries.
- More difficult to benefit from purchasing economies of scale.
- Harder to react to sudden changes in demand or large one-off orders.

Just in case (JIC)

JIC means a business will hold **buffer stock** in case it is needed. Holding a minimum amount of stock will help to protect the business from any delays in supplies and will help them to meet unexpected orders. It also means that they do not need to receive as many deliveries, which can save the business money.

Benefits

- Can continue to produce when there are delays in supplies.
- Can meet unexpected surges in demand, or one-off large orders.
- Can benefit from bulk-buying discounts.

Drawbacks

- Have to pay for storage of buffer stock which can be costly.
- Increased risk that stock gets wasted (if perishable), stolen or damaged.
- Requires warehouse management and stock control.

THE ROLE OF PROCUREMENT

Procurement is the term used to describe the process a business goes through in finding and obtaining the right materials and supplies to be used in the production process.

Effects of procurement and logistics

The process of procurement involves the following stages:

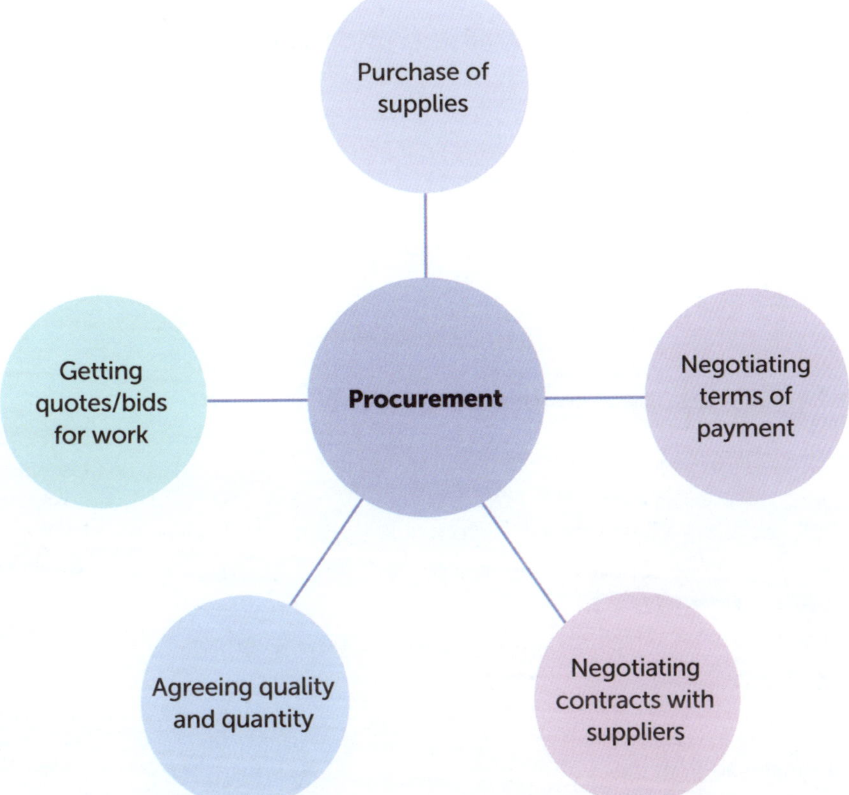

Logistics refers to the management of supplies and finished products throughout the **supply chain**, in order to ensure that deliveries arrive on time for the production process. It is also concerned with ensuring that deliveries of finished goods to customers are timely.

State and explain **two** impacts that effective procurement and logistics can have on a business. [4]

One impact is that the business can become more efficient.[1] This is because by having good logistics, delivery of any raw materials to be used in production won't be delayed.[1]

Another impact is that the business could have lower unit costs,[1] because effective procurement will involve negotiation of better deals for its supplies.[1]

SUPPLY CHAIN MANAGEMENT

The **supply chain** describes how businesses produce and distribute goods and services. It also refers to all the people, activities and businesses involved in the whole process. A key part of an effective supply chain is choosing the right supplier.

Factors affecting the choice of suppliers

If a business can find the right supplier, the production process can become more efficient.

The right supplier:

- will supply the best **quality** materials at the best possible **price**.
- will negotiate their own prices so that trade customers can make cost savings, particularly when buying in bulk, or where there is a long-standing relationship.
- will be flexible, quick and **reliable** in delivery so that the business gets the right supplies, at the right time, avoiding stoppages in production or sales.
- has the materials that a business needs in stock.
- can be trusted.
- offers favourable payment terms.

Value of effective supply chain management

By effectively managing the supply chain, a business can benefit in the following ways:

- Delivery from suppliers will be on time and processes will run efficiently.
- The business will receive supplies at the best possible price, enabling them to lower their own price to customers.
- Waste will be minimised, which can also enable faster production times.

Remember: The benefits of reduced costs must be balanced against the quality of a product.

Explain **one** impact on a business when purchasing raw materials from the cheapest supplier. [2]

Using a cheaper supplier may mean that the quality of materials is lower.[1] *This may impact the overall quality of the finished product which could upset customers.*[1]

THE CONCEPT OF QUALITY

A business' goods and services must be of a sufficient quality to satisfy customers' needs and wants. If quality falls short of these expectations, then the business could suffer as a result.

Consequences of quality issues

If a business produces a product or service which does not meet the standards expected by customers, then the business could suffer from the following consequences:

Customer complaints

Customers who are not happy will complain to the business and may leave negative reviews. They are also likely to tell others of their poor experience. This can impact the business' reputation.

Returned products

If there is an issue with a product, customers may return the product to the business. This will increase costs as the business must restock, repair or replace the faulty product.

Loss of customers

If a customer has a bad experience with a product, they will be less likely to use that business again.

Lower selling price

If a business gets a reputation for having quality issues, customers will not pay a lot for their products. Therefore, they may have to lower their prices.

Wasted resources

If there is a fault in a batch of products, they may have to be disposed of, which will increase waste. There may also be a lot of products left unsold.

Legal action

Depending on the circumstances, a customer could sue a business for selling faulty or dangerous products.

Give **two** ways in which a business can identify product quality issues. [2]

Two from: Through questioning customers and receiving their feedback.[1] *By asking employees.*[1] *Mystery shopping.*[1] *Checking production data / quality control processes.*[1]

MAINTAINING QUALITY

Businesses can prevent quality issues from becoming a problem in many ways. One of the most common methods is by adopting a **Total Quality Management** approach during the production process.

Total quality management (TQM)

TQM puts quality at the heart of a business' culture. It emphasises achieving quality in all aspects of an organisation. All employees are responsible for ensuring their work is of the highest quality. When work is passed from one employee to another, the person that is receiving the work is seen as an internal customer. It is a system designed to prevent mistakes from happening, rather than having to fix them later on.

A business would introduce TQM in order to benefit from the following:

Fewer defective products

As everyone takes responsibility for the quality of their work, they should not be moving it through production if there are quality issues. This should, in theory, eliminate all defects.

Increased levels of motivation

As staff are given more responsibility, they may feel more valued by the business. Their work matters. This can be motivating for staff, who may become more productive as a result.

Reduced costs

As there should be a reduction in the amount of wasted products, the business should experience lower costs, which can mean that they are able to lower the price of the product, or maintain price levels and enjoy higher profit margins per unit. It is also more efficient to iron out faults in production before they reach the customer, than to go back and fix them later on. A **product recall** can be very expensive and damaging to reputation.

1. Explain **one** drawback to a business from introducing a system of total quality management. [2]

   A business may have to train workers to take on the responsibility of checking the quality of their work.[1] This can increase costs which may eliminate any cost savings.[1]

Costs and benefits of maintaining quality

A business can maintain a high standard of quality by employing the following methods:

- Train staff so that they are better at their jobs and therefore produce a higher quality standard of work.
- Ensure that they use suppliers that deliver materials of sufficient quality that match the quality expectations of the business and its customers.
- Involve staff in discussions about how systems and processes can be improved.
- Invest in better technology to help improve standards of production.

Maintaining quality can help a business to achieve a competitive advantage but they must be aware of the costs of doing so.

Benefits

- **Good brand image** – If a business becomes known for having good quality products, then they will experience **reputational benefits**.
- **Increased sales** – If a business gains a reputation for high quality, then more customers are likely to purchase from them.
- **Higher price** – Having a high quality product is a source of added value, meaning customers will be willing to pay a higher price for them.

Costs

- **Staff training** – To ensure staff have the necessary skills to produce work of the required standard, they will need training which can add to the costs of the business.
- **Inspection costs** – Monitoring and inspecting the quality of products can be expensive and time consuming.
- **Maintaining standards through growth** – As businesses become larger it becomes more difficult to achieve consistent quality.

2. Explain **two** reasons why a business may struggle to maintain quality standards as it grows. [4]

One reason is because a business may decide to offer franchises to franchisees,[1] therefore they lose some control over monitoring the quality of the product.[1]

Another reason is that a business may decide to grow quickly by outsourcing its production.[1] This will mean that the business no longer has responsibility for the production process and the third-party business may not have the same high expectations in terms of quality.[1]

GOOD CUSTOMER SERVICES

Offering good customer service is one way that a business can gain an advantage over competitors. By looking after customers, a business will gain a good reputation that will help them to be successful.

Methods of good service

Product knowledge

Being able to answer customer questions with detail and confidence will help them determine which good or service is most suitable for fulfilling their needs. It will make a customer feel more reassured when purchasing from a business that really understands what it offers.

Customer engagement

Any interaction between the customer and the business needs to be a **positive experience** in order to make them want to further engage with the business. Making the customer feel valued will enhance their experience and ensure that they know that the business cares about them.

Post-sales service

A customer's experience with a business does not finish when they purchase a product. For some businesses, the service the customer receives afterwards is just as important. Businesses can offer **user training** for technological products; they could offer **help lines** that customers can call if they have a question, and they can also offer **servicing** and maintenance of the product.

Benefits of good customer service

- Increased customer satisfaction
- Customers purchase more products
- Greater chance of making profit
- Customers become loyal
- Source of competitive advantage
- Source of added value

Dangers of poor customer service

A business can be seriously harmed if they provide poor customer service. They could:

- Cause **customer dissatisfaction**.
- Gain a **poor reputation** via word of mouth.
- See a **fall in sales** and profits.

Identify and explain **two** dangers to a business of providing poor customer service. [4]

One danger is that customers may become dissatisfied.[1] *As a result, they may decide to purchase from a competitor instead.*[1]

A second danger is that a business could gain a poor reputation as customers leave bad reviews and tell their friends and family about their negative experience.[1] *Therefore it could see a fall in sales and revenue.*[1]

Ways in which ICT have developed customer services

Advancements in **information and communications technologies** (**ICT**) have enabled businesses to develop their customer services through the following methods:

Websites

Most businesses will have some sort of a website. Websites allow businesses to detail information about their products and services, including the presentation of pictures and videos, to customers. They can also include a section with frequently asked questions, allowing customers to find out the answers to queries they may have.

E-commerce

Selling products online increases the convenience for the customer as they can purchase at a time that is suitable for them, and in the comfort of their own home. E-commerce also allows customers to research products without any sales pressure, and to read reviews from previous customers; all of which will help them to make an informed buying decision.

Social media

Businesses can collect a wide range of customer views on social media. Interacting with customers in this way allows the business to gain a deeper understanding of their wants, needs and general opinions because customers can post comments, reviews and videos. Not only does the use of such apps allow a business to gain feedback, they can also monitor whether customers are satisfied by looking at ratings and reading details of customer experiences.

SweetDelights Ltd is a well-established factory specialising in the production of a variety of sweets. The manufacturer has recently introduced new technology to the production process and now uses flow production to mass produce its sweets. It has also recently adopted a just-in-time approach to stock control to help become more efficient.

With increasing demand for their products, the company is facing a critical decision regarding the selection of a supplier for one of its key ingredients. SweetDelights Ltd relies on a specific ingredient, SugarX, to manufacture its signature sweets. Currently, the company has been sourcing SugarX from Supplier A for the past five years. However, due to changing market dynamics, SweetDelights Ltd is exploring the possibility of switching to Supplier B, which has recently entered the market with competitive pricing and claims of superior product quality.

SweetDelights Ltd has done some research on the two suppliers:

Costs	• Supplier A has been a reliable partner for several years, offering consistent quality at a reasonable price. • Supplier B, while relatively new, is offering a lower price for SugarX, creating the potential for cost savings.
Quality	• SweetDelights Ltd has built a reputation for high-quality sweets, and any compromise in the quality of SugarX may impact the final product. • Supplier B claims to have a more advanced production process, resulting in a higher quality SugarX.
Reliability and delivery time	• Supplier A has a proven track record of timely deliveries, ensuring that SweetDelights Ltd can meet customer demand consistently. • Supplier B is relatively untested in terms of reliability and may pose a risk in terms of meeting production schedules.
Relationship and loyalty	• SweetDelights Ltd values the long-standing relationship with Supplier A and acknowledges the importance of loyalty in business partnerships. • Shifting to Supplier B might strain relationships with Supplier A and could impact future collaborations.

The management at SweetDelights Ltd is faced with a challenging decision. The company must weigh the benefits of cost savings and potential quality improvement against the risks of disrupting a longstanding relationship with Supplier A.

EXAMINATION PRACTICE

1. Which **one** of the following is **not** a stage of the procurement process? [1]
   A – Getting quotes from suppliers
   B – Giving good customer service
   C – Negotiating terms of payment
   D – Selecting suppliers

2. Which **one** of the following is a benefit of introducing a TQM system? [1]
   A – Charging a higher price
   B – Fewer defective products
   C – Increased costs
   D – Reduced levels of motivation

3. Explain **one** way in which ICT has impacted customer service. [2]

4. Explain **one** benefit to a business from engaging in lean production. [2]

5. Explain **one** benefit to a business of having effective supply chain management. [2]

For the following questions, you must refer to Case study 3 on the previous page.

6. Explain **one** drawback to SweetDelights Ltd from using a just in time system of stock control. [4]

7. Explain **one** way in which SweetDelights Ltd can offer good customer service. [4]

8. Analyse the impact on SweetDelights Ltd from using flow production. [6]

9. Analyse the importance to SweetDelights Ltd of having a quality product. [6]

10. The management at SweetDelights Ltd. is faced with a challenging decision. The company must weigh up the benefits of cost savings and potential quality improvement against the risks of disrupting a longstanding relationship with Supplier A.
    Recommend whether SweetDelights Ltd should remain with Supplier A or change to Supplier B. [9]

ORGANISATIONAL STRUCTURES

An **organisational structure** refers to the way in which a business is organised in terms of its employees. The structure selected by a business will impact issues such as employee motivation and communication.

Organisational structure

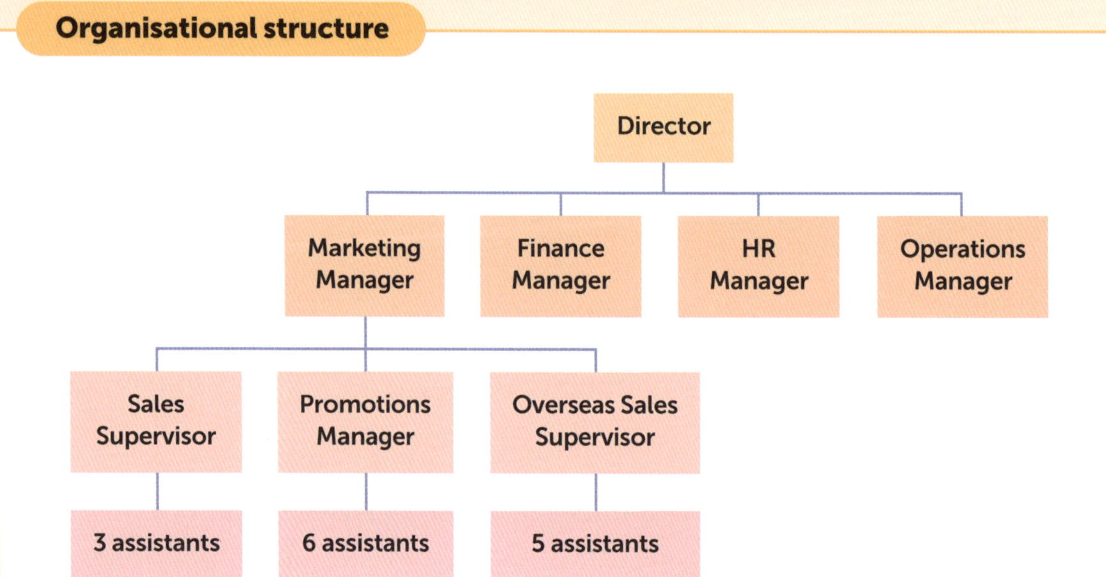

Span of control

The **span of control** is the number of people that a line manager is directly responsible for. A wide span of control means a manager has many subordinates to manage. In the example above, the Marketing Manager has a span of control of 3 that they are directly responsible for.

Delayering

Delayering involves reducing the number of levels within the hierarchy by removing elements from the organisational structure. The reason for this would be to reduce costs or to improve the speed and quality of communication, as the chain of command would become shorter.

Chain of command

The **chain of command** is the line of authority within a business along which communication passes. For instance, in the example above, if the Director wanted to pass details of new marketing objectives for the business, they will pass instructions to the Marketing Manager. In turn, they would then pass these on to the Supervisors, who would then inform the assistants they are responsible for. Effective communication becomes more difficult as the chain gets longer.

Delegation

Delegation means to pass authority and responsibility to colleagues lower down in the hierarchy. For instance, in the example above, the Director may delegate all decisions regarding marketing, to the Marketing Manager.

Reasons for having an organisational structure

As a business grows, it becomes increasingly important to have a defined internal structure for the following reasons:

It helps to improve the flow of communication: Having an internal structure makes the chain of command obvious. Therefore, channels of communications are clearly defined.

Allows a business to function: An organisational structure will separate employees into functional areas, ensuring that all necessary aspects of business are covered.

Allows a business to organise its employees: Employees will understand their roles better in relation to other colleagues.

It shows how employees fit into the business: Employees can immediately see who their line manager is and which others they are responsible for.

It helps in monitoring employees: All managers will know who they are responsible for, therefore they can ensure they support and guide their subordinates.

Job roles and responsibilities

Having an internal structure allows a business to have clearly defined roles and responsibilities.

CEO: The Chief Executive Officer has the most authority in the business and will lead the board of directors.

Directors: Directors are responsible for making decisions on the long-term strategy of the business and how they will achieve success. They are responsible for the managers.

Managers: Managers will be responsible for determining how their functional area will help to achieve the business' long term goals. They will be responsible for the day to day running of their area.

Supervisors: Supervisors (team leaders) will directly oversee a number of shop floor workers. They will report to the managers. They will support managers in achieving their targets, but also support shop floor workers in carrying out their activities.

Shop floor workers: Workers carry out the business' everyday activities. If it is a manufacturing business, then they will work on the production line. If it is a café, then they will prepare the food and serve the customers.

Explain how delayering could cause issues with the span of control. [2]

Removing a layer from the organisational structure would mean that some staff would become responsible for more people.[1] If a someone is responsible for too many others, they will be unable to monitor their work effectively and mistakes could happen.[1]

DIFFERENT TYPES OF ORGANISATIONAL STRUCTURES

Tall vs flat structure

Tall structure

- Many levels of hierarchy, therefore a longer chain of command.
- Promotional opportunities for staff.
- Managers have a narrow span of control.
- Slower communication flow.

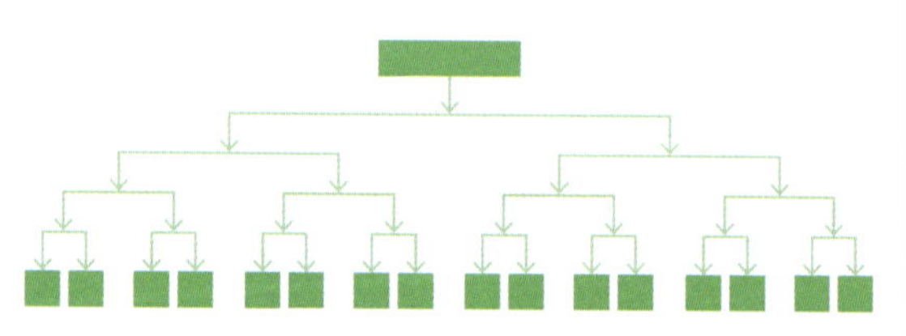

Flat structure

- Fewer levels of hierarchy, so there will be a shorter chain of command.
- Managers have wide spans of control.
- More delegation and authority given to staff.
- Communication is quicker as there are fewer levels in the hierarchy.

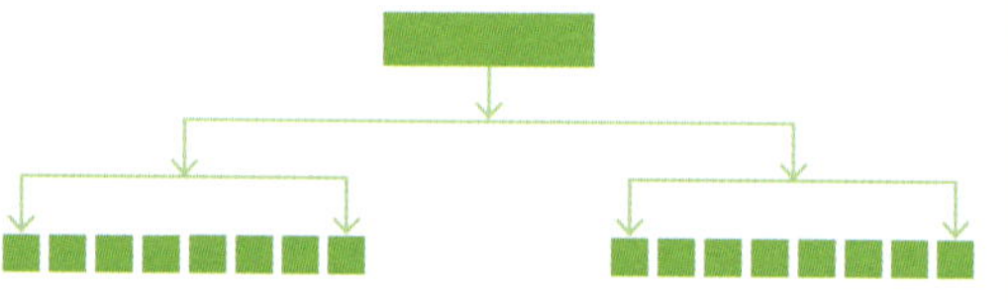

Centralised vs Decentralised structures

Centralised

A **centralised** business structure keeps the main decision-making powers with the senior management team, often based in the business' headquarters. Under this system, all local branches of the business will look the same, sell the same products and charge the same amount. The main advantage is that senior managers should have lots of experience in making difficult decisions and the customer knows exactly what to expect, regardless of which branch they visit.

Decentralised

Under a **decentralised** structure, decision making powers are delegated to the local managers. The rationale behind this is that these managers know their local market better than the senior managers. As local employees have the authority to make decisions, they can be made quicker as approval from those above them in the hierarchy is not needed.

Explain **one** drawback to a business of having a decentralised structure. [2]

The reputation of the firm may be damaged by the actions of one branch.[1] This is because the local managers can make their own decisions on what to sell and how to price it. If they sell a product that is not consistent with the quality of the firm, it won't only be that branch that gains a negative image, but the business as a whole.[1]

RECRUITMENT AND SELECTION OF EMPLOYEES

When recruiting, a business must decide what role it needs to fill and what method they will use to recruit those required.

The need for recruitment

A business may need to recruit a new employee for one of the following reasons:

- When a business first becomes established.
- The business is growing.
- Replacing an employee that has left. This could be because they have accepted another job elsewhere or they have retired.
- The current workforce does not possess the skills that the business needs.
- To cover a position on a temporary basis. An employee could be on maternity/paternity leave or could be on long term sickness absence.

Internal and external recruitment

Internal recruitment means a vacancy is filled by someone who already works in the business. **External recruitment** occurs when a business employs someone who does not already work for the organisation. The benefits of each method are detailed below:

Internal

- The candidate will already know the business and the business will know them, so less induction training is needed.
- Faster, easier and cheaper way to recruit.
- Promoting from within can be motivating for employees.

External

- New employees may bring fresh ideas.
- There may be a bigger pool of potential applicants to choose from.
- May be necessary to use if the vacancy has arisen due to growth of the business.

1. Explain **one** drawback of externally recruiting an employee. [2]
2. Explain **one** drawback of internal recruitment to a business. [2]

1. *The business will know less about the person they select than if they had recruited internally.*[1] *Therefore, they have a greater chance of making a mistake with the selection.*[1]
2. *The pool of internal employees may not have the exact skills that the business needs.*[1] *Therefore, they may have to pay more to train the employee who is selected for the role.*[1]

RECRUITMENT AND SELECTION PROCESS

Recruitment is the process of finding potential employees who may be suitable for the position, while **selection** is the act of choosing the most suitable candidate to fulfil the vacant role.

Stages of recruitment

The recruitment and selection process involves the following stages:

1	**Job analysis**	This is the process of collecting and interpreting information about a job, so the business knows what tasks it involves and what skills will be needed.
2	**Write a job description**	A document detailing the duties the employee will undertake in the job is drawn up from the findings of the job analysis.
3	**Write a person specification**	A document outlining the qualifications, qualities and attributes required. To be shortlisted, a candidate should possess these.
4	**Advertise the job**	Information about the job and application details are advertised. Where and how a job is advertised will be dependent on what the job is and the location of potential employees.
5	**Send / receive applications / CVs**	Application forms created by the business are completed by the applicants, who may also send in a CV.
6	**Shortlist**	After the closing date, the business will remove unsuitable applicants from the list and the best ones will be shortlisted for interview.
7	**Interviews and testing**	At interview, shortlisted candidates are questioned and may undertake some form of testing, this could be skill specific or personality based.
8	**Selection and references**	The best candidate is selected for the job and references checked.

Identify and explain **two** benefits to a business from having an effective recruitment and selection process. [4]

A business may experience high levels of productivity.[1] If a business employs the right workers with the right skills, they will be able to produce more products per hour.[1]

A business can experience higher levels of staff retention / greater staff motivation.[1] This is because staff will be happier in their roles when they are more suitable for them, so they are less likely to want to leave.[1]

A business may achieve a higher quality of output / better customer service,[1] because the skills of the recruits will have been well-matched to the role through job analysis.[1]

CONTRACTS OF EMPLOYMENT

Many businesses are changing the way they ask employees to work. Flexible working arrangements are much more common, and this can suit both the individual and the business.

Full and part-time employment

Full-time

A **full-time employee** is usually classed as someone who works a standard number of hours a week. This number differs from business to business but is usually between 35 and 40 hours. (an individual cannot work more than 48 hours per week due to regulations in place). A business benefits as the employer may gain more experience more quickly because they ultimately work more hours a week, giving them greater opportunity to learn and improve their performance. It can also improve customer service, for example, if the same person is available for customers as a point of contact every day of the week.

Part-time

A **part-time employee** has exactly the same rights as a full-time member of staff but works less than the standard number of hours per week. A business may benefit as they have enough staff for the busy periods, for example weekends, but are not overstaffed at quieter times.

Job share

Job share is where an employee shares the responsibility of a single job with another employee.

Explain **one** reason why a business may offer a job share. [2]

This could bring a wider range of skills to the business.[1] This is because the business will employ two people on a part-time basis to work one full-time job, so they benefit from the skills of both employees.[1]

It offers an opportunity to retain two high performing staff members[1] who require more flexibility in their working hours / personal circumstances have changed.[1]

Zero-hour contracts

Zero-hours contracts are provided where there are no guaranteed hours for a worker. These arrangements are often used in businesses with large fluctuations in demand, for example peak Christmas shopping. It allows a business to keep costs to a minimum as they only pay workers as they are required. It also allows workers the flexibility to work only when it is convenient for them. When offered working hours, the worker does not have to accept the work offered.

MOTIVATING EMPLOYEES

Motivation can be defined as the reason an employee acts or behaves in a certain way. It is their desire or willingness to complete a task. To be successful, a business needs motivated staff who can be enthused or encouraged using financial or non-financial methods.

Importance of motivation in the workforce

Motivation is important for a number of reasons:

- **Staff retention** is increased. This lowers staff turnover which is a measure of the percentage of the workforce who leave over a period of time.
- Staff absence rates may be lower as employees enjoy coming to work.
- It helps to attract new employees. People will want to come and work for a business that looks after them.
- Happier and more motivated employees are likely to provide better customer service, enhancing the business' reputation.
- A more committed workforce will want to be involved in helping the business succeed; as a result they may be more likely to provide new ideas.
- It can help to improve communication within the business.
- The **productivity** of a business may increase.

Methods to motivate staff

Financial methods of motivation

Salary

A **salary** is a fixed amount paid per year, usually split into monthly payments. Paying an employee a high salary can be motivating, but employees are also motivated by the prospect of incremental increases in salary over time.

Commission

Commission usually forms part of a financial package for sales staff. For every sale made, the employee will receive a percentage of that sale as **bonus** income. Therefore, they are motivated to sell as much as possible, which also benefits the business financially.

Wage

A **wage** is usually paid weekly to an employee in return for a set number of hours of work. Employees paid by this method may be motivated to work **overtime** as they will then often receive an enhanced hourly rate for their efforts.

Profit sharing

A **profit share** agreement financially rewards employees with a share of the business' profits alongside their usual salary or wage. They will be motivated to help the business perform better in order to increase the value of their share of the profits.

Non-financial methods of motivation

Styles of management

Some managers will retain the authority to make decisions and keep tight control for themselves. Others will adapt their **management style** with greater delegation to allow more junior employees to have the authority to make decisions themselves. This can be motivating because employees feel valued and trusted by the business.

Greater responsibility

This is achieved through **job enrichment**, which is the act of varying tasks or delegating greater decision making to others. This will motivate an employee because it provides a new challenge and makes them feel valued by the business. It also reduces boredom.

Training

Training can be motivating as it allows employees to learn new skills. People commonly feel more loyal to a business that invests time and money into developing them. They feel valued and that the business believes in them, which can improve their productivity. Training is covered in more detail on **page 58**.

Fringe benefits

Fringe benefits are often called 'perks'. They are additional benefits provided by a business to an employee.

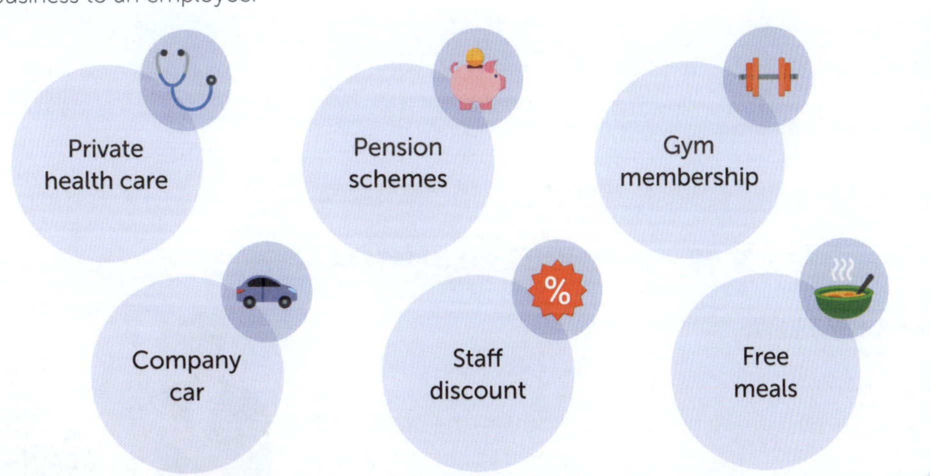

Explain **one** way in which fringe benefits motivate employees. [2]

Fringe benefits are motivational because they are additional perks given to employees on top of their wage / salary.[1] An example is offering an employee discount when buying the business' own products so they feel happier that they can buy them for less money.[1]

TRAINING

Developing an employee not only benefits the individual but also has its advantages for the business. Training can take many forms, but it is essential that all businesses conduct necessary ongoing training so that employees can keep up to date with the latest developments.

Importance of training the workforce

Increased productivity: Training workers will enhance their skills and knowledge and therefore to make them better at their jobs. This will increase efficiency and productivity where more work is completed in the same amount of time.

Ability to deal with changes in technology: Technology is constantly changing, and most jobs will involve the use of some sort of technology. Training employees in the use of new systems and techniques will help to keep them efficient and productive in their work.

Production of high-quality goods: Skilled employees with a knowledge of quality control will produce a better product with fewer mistakes.

Good customer service: Well-informed employees are much more likely to deal with customers in an effective way, making sure that the customer's needs are fully met.

Staff retention: Employees who feel valued by a business are less likely to leave. Employees may also appreciate the training and development they are getting in their career, further increasing their loyalty and commitment to the business.

Motivation: By investing in training a member of staff, a business is giving that employee the opportunity to learn new skills and develop themselves. This can be extremely motivating as they may feel valued by the business.

Types of training undertaken by businesses

Induction training

Induction training takes place when someone is new to a job. It allows them to become familiar with the business and its processes, as well as having an introduction to the role that they will be fulfilling. The benefit of this training is that:

- It allows an employee to understand what they need to do in their role. This helps to ensure that they become productive sooner.

- It helps a new employee to settle quickly so they feel more confident, more secure and less likely to leave.

On the job training

On the job training is usually conducted whilst the employee is undertaking their normal daily tasks. It is delivered by other, more experienced, members of staff.

Benefits	Drawbacks
• Training can be tailored to the individual, and will meet the exact needs of the business. • It is a cheaper way to train people. • The individual is contributing whilst training.	• Unlikely to generate new ideas into the business. • Having to train whilst undertaking a job you are not fully trained in can be stressful. • Can take more experienced workers away from their own work as they provide the training.

Off the job training

Off the job training is training that staff attend away from their place of work, often in colleges or training centres.

Benefits	Drawbacks
• Training is delivered by specialists. • Usually highly structured and may provide the employee with a qualification. • Can generate fresh ideas into a business.	• Attending training courses can be expensive. • Can take employees away from their work. • Upskilled employees become more attractive to rival businesses offering higher pay.

Case study

Bella Cucina Bistro has three outlets and is known for its authentic Italian cuisine. The sudden departure of the Finance Manager left the management in a tight spot. The responsibility for managing accounts fell on the shoulders of Marco Rossi, a senior staff member, with no previous accounts experience except what he had learned as part of his Business degree. The management also had to organise the training of new wait staff to work in the newly opened third bistro. Sofia Bianchi, an experienced shift manager, was tasked with sorting out the training for these employees.

In the exam you may have to recommend which type of training is suitable in the circumstances laid out in the case study. Think what would be appropriate, for example off the job training for Marco would be best so that he could complete an Accounts qualification, whereas the new wait staff would benefit from on-the-job training where they could shadow the experienced shift manager.

SkyLink Express Ltd are a budget airline connecting passengers between Europe and the USA. The organisational structure is very tall. It includes many levels with decision-makers sat at the top in the London head office. Managers hold the reins tightly, making decisions that cascade down, impacting pilots and cabin crew across the company.

SkyLink Express face difficulties with staffing, particularly with a shortage of cabin crew. Many have gone to work for a rival airline that offered more enticing packages. In response, SkyLink Express initiated a recruitment drive, seeking to find fresh faces eager to have a career in the skies. To motivate the cabin crew, SkyLink Express currently offer a basic salary to provide financial stability, and an additional hourly rate awarded for the time they spend in the air.

In an effort to cut costs further, SkyLink Express is contemplating elevating the hourly rate for cabin crew and the introduction of zero-hours contracts. This move stirred a mix of apprehension and discontent among the flight attendants, although they would be better financially rewarded when working, job security would become uncertain in the face of fluctuating schedules.

To be allowed to fly, new recruits must undertake induction training which includes a blend of safety protocols, customer service essentials, and resilience-exercises to prepare them for unpredictable events in budget airline aviation.

EXAMINATION PRACTICE

1. Which **one** of the following would be included in a person specification?   [1]
    A – Details of the pay that the successful candidate will receive.
    B – Information on the location where the successful candidate will be working.
    C – Qualifications that are necessary to carry out the job.
    D – Responsibilities that come with the job.

2. Which **one** of the following best describes 'span of control'?   [1]
    A – The line of authority within a business along which communication passes.
    B – The number of people that a line manager is directly responsible for.
    C – The passing down of authority to employees lower down in the hierarchy.
    D – The removal of levels within the hierarchy or organisational structure.

3. Explain **one** reason why it is important for a growing business to have an organisational structure. [2]

4. Explain **one** benefit to a business from adopting a decentralised structure.   [2]

5. Explain **one** benefit to a business from recruiting externally.   [2]

6. Explain **one** benefit to a business from on the job training.   [2]

For the following questions, you must refer to Case study 4 on the previous page.

7. Explain **one** benefit to SkyLink Express of having a motivated workforce.   [4]

8. Explain **one** benefit to SkyLink Express of having an effective recruitment and
    selection process.   [4]

9. Analyse the impacts on SkyLink Express of having a tall hierarchy.   [6]

10. Analyse the reasons why SkyLink Express carry out induction training.   [6]

11. Recommend whether SkyLink Express should introduce the zero hours contracts for
    cabin crew.   [9]

IDENTIFYING AND UNDERSTANDING CUSTOMERS

Businesses must meet customer needs if they are to be successful.

The importance of identifying and satisfying customer needs

Ultimately, a business must identify and meet the needs of their customers in order to survive. Identifying customer needs allows a business:

To provide a product or service that the customer would buy

People buy things that solve problems for them. If a business didn't find out what customers need, then they might produce a product that no-one wants to purchase.

To select the right marketing mix

Identifying customer needs will mean that the business knows exactly what the product should be, what price to sell it at, where it needs to be distributed to and how best to promote it.

To increase sales

When their needs have been met, satisfied customers are likely to return to the business. Therefore, they become loyal and purchase again. This causes sales to increase.

To avoid costly mistakes

If a business provides a product that doesn't fit customers' needs then they will not buy it. The business may have spent a large amount of money producing a product or wasting resources on something that earns them no revenue in return. This can be a cause of failure for a business.

To be competitive

Goods or services that clearly meet a customer's needs will have a competitive edge over those that only meet some needs. This can also represent better value for money if priced competitively.

SEGMENTATION

Market segmentation involves grouping customers together based on shared characteristics, wants and needs. Once the target segment is decided upon, the business must decide what their needs are and where to place their product in the market.

How a business segments the market

Location

Grouping customers together based on where they live enables a business to focus on selling to people in certain areas.

Lifestyle

Grouping customers based on their hobbies and interests or based on the way they live their lives (e.g. health conscious and active) can help identify more relevant customers.

Age

Grouping customers based on how old they are.

Gender

A business may decide to segment the market based on gender, as it is common that they have different needs.

Income

People can be grouped by income bracket (how much money they earn). A product may be more suitable for a budget or luxury market.

Why businesses segment the market

To promote the product more effectively: The business can promote in places where their target market will notice them. For instance, a company selling golf clubs can place an advert in a golf magazine.

To develop products that fit a specific groups' needs: A business may be able to charge more for a niche product, as customers will be willing to pay more for a product that is specifically targeted at them, e.g. hearing aids or invisible dental braces.

To differentiate from competitors: Offering a product that meets the specific needs of a group of customers will help a business stand out from its rivals.

Explain **two** drawbacks to a business of segmenting the market. [4]

One drawback to a business is that the market will become narrower.[1] This means that the business will restrict the number of potential customers that it is aiming at.[1]

Another drawback is that it can be more expensive to segment the market.[1] This is because they will have to adapt their product to meet the individual needs of the segment they are aiming at.[1]

THE PURPOSE AND METHODS OF MARKET RESEARCH

Satisfying customer needs is the key to success. One of the key reasons for carrying out **market research** is to identify market opportunities. It will also give a business data on the market itself and potential competitors.

Purpose of market research

A business will research the market for the following reasons:

To establish demand

Market research can help establish whether there will be sufficient **demand** for a product. Without finding out this information, a business may produce a product that nobody wants.

To identify the target market

By researching customers, a business can find out who fits the likely **target market**, and what characteristics they share. This will help them to make decisions about their **marketing mix** (see more information on this in **specification section 3.5.4**)

To gain an understanding of the competition

By looking at what else is available in the market, a business can find out if there are other businesses that are selling similar products. If there are not, then the business may have found a **gap in the market**. Otherwise, it can ascertain what other products are selling and therefore produce something that is unique. A business can also find out what price **competitors** charge, what promotion they undertake and where its products are sold.

Qualitative and quantitative data

Qualitative data is based on people's feelings, judgements and opinions, and cannot be expressed in numerical form. **Quantitative data** is numerical and therefore can be statistically analysed more easily.

Market research will be more effective when a business uses a combination of both quantitative and qualitative data. Managers need to be able to explain the statistics and figures that have been collected. Qualitative data allows them to do this.

Explain **one** impact of making decisions based on unreliable market research data. [4]

If a business has unreliable data, then they may produce a product that isn't wanted.[1] This could be because they have not surveyed a representative sample of their target market.[1] This could mean a lot of money is wasted in producing these products,[1] causing the business to have cash flow problems.[1]

Primary market research is new information that is collected first-hand by a business. It includes carrying out a **survey**, asking people to fill out a **questionnaire**, undertaking an **interview** with a potential customer and holding **focus groups**.

Benefits

- The information collected will be up to date.
- The questions asked can be tailored to the business conducting the research.
- It allows a business to have direct contact with existing and potential customers.

Drawbacks

- It can be time consuming to collect.
- The research is open to potential bias, depending on the sample used.
- Often more expensive.

Survey: A method of gathering information by asking relevant questions of potential customers.

Questionnaire: A type of survey whereby a set of questions are distributed (in commonly larger numbers) by mail, online or in person, for potential customers to fill in. Quantitative data will usually be collected.

Interview: A further type of survey whereby an interviewer asks in depth questions either by phone or in person. This allows a business to gain detailed qualitative information, but there will be a smaller sample size as interviews are more time-consuming and expensive to conduct.

Focus group: A small group of people who are selected to give their opinions on a particular product or aspect of a business. Follow up questions can be asked to gain valuable additional detail, but only a limited number of people will be involved which may not always be completely reflective of the whole target market. Focus groups are time-consuming to arrange and conduct, and participants will usually need to be paid a fee for their attendance.

Secondary market research

Secondary market research involves gathering data that already exists as it has been collected by someone else. Examples include researching on the **Internet** and looking at **printed press**.

Benefits

- It is usually cheaper than primary research.
- It can be less time consuming because information is more easily found.

Drawbacks

- The information gathered may not be specific or relevant to the business.
- The information may be out of date.

Internet research: Used to find information from websites including government and competitor sites.

Printed press: A business could carry out research by reading newspapers and published journals.

USE OF MARKET RESEARCH DATA

Businesses will use the information and data that has been collected to help inform decision making. The data should provide details on the size of the overall market, allowing them to understand their **market share**.

Market size

Market size can be measured in two ways – by value or volume. Volume refers to the total number of products sold, whereas value refers to the total amount of income generated in a market from the sales of similar products by all competitors. It can be calculated using the formula:

Market size = total number of products sold × average selling price per product sold

Market share

Market share is defined as the percentage of the total sales made in a market by one business. It can be calculated using the formula:

Market share = (sales of the product ÷ total market sales) × 100

1. The Fisher King is a fish and chip shop that has been trading for just over two years. Year 1 sales were £32,400. The total sales in the market for Year 1 were £180,000. In Year 2, the management conducted market research to estimate the sales figures of their rivals to see how their sales levels compare. The sales figures for all the fish and chip shops in the market in Year 2 are as follows:

   - The Fisher King – £37,500
   - Salt Delish – £25,400
   - Catch 'n' fry – £42,750
   - The Fish and Chip Stop – £39,000
   - Aqua Nosh – £26,000

   (a) Calculate the market size in Year 2, by value. [2]

   (b) Calculate the change in Fisher King's market share from Year 1 to Year 2.

   Show your workings. [3]

   (a) Total sales in the market = 37,500 + 25,400 + 42,750 + 39,000 + 26,000[1] = £170,650 [1]

   (b) Market share Year 2 = (37,500 ÷ 170,650) × 100 = 21.97% (Allow 22%) [1]

   Market share Year 1 = (32,400 ÷ 180,000) × 100 = 18% [1]

   Change in market share = 21.97 – 18.00 = +3.97% (Allow 4%) [1]

The AQA specification stipulates that you will have to manipulate and interpret data from tables and charts. These charts could take many different forms, so make sure you understand what information is being presented.

2. A pie chart showing the market share of the fish and chip shops in Year 1 is given below. The market size by value was £180,000 in that year.

(a) Use the information in the chart and the sales figures for The Fisher King in Year 2, in question 1, to calculate the change in sales in Year 2 as a percentage of their Year 1 sales. [3]

**Market share in the
fish and chip market in Year 1**

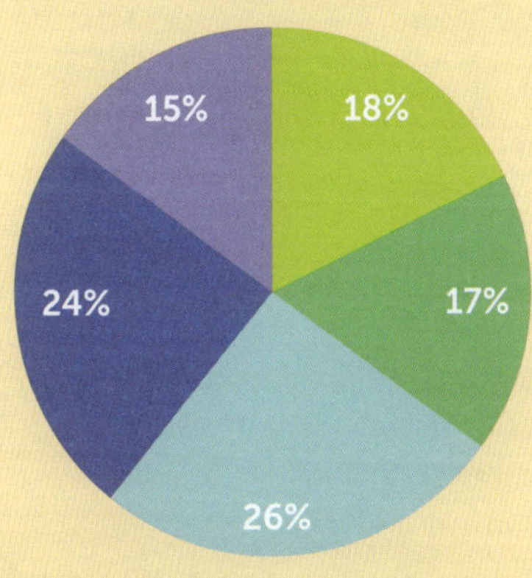

(b) Explain what this means for The Fisher King's performance in Year 2. [4]

(a) *Sales in Year 1 = 180,000 × 18% = £32,400. (Given in question 1.)*

Change in sales = 37,500 − 32,400 = Reduction of £5,100 [1]

Change as a percentage = (5200 ÷ 32,400) × 100 [1] *= Reduction of 16.05%* [1]

(b) *Sales performance fell in Year 2 compared to year 1* [✓] *even though Fisher King's market share rose* [✓] *because total sales for the whole market were lower in Year 2 than in Year 1.* [✓] *So, compared to their competitors, Fisher King may have performed relatively well, attracting a greater percentage of customers Year 2, even with an overall fall in sales.* [✓]

THE MARKETING MIX: PRICE

The price a business charges plays an important role in developing a successful marketing mix. A business must choose which pricing strategy to adopt, but there are many factors that will influence this decision.

Pricing methods

There is a basic relationship between price and demand: As prices rise, demand is likely to fall.

Price skimming

A business will set a high price for its product as it is launched into the market. This may be because it is a technologically superior product, of higher quality than the rest of the market, or it is highly differentiated in some way, meaning people are prepared to pay more for it.

Competitive pricing

A business will set a price for its products based on the price that rival businesses charge. They will commonly match the price of their rivals, or just undercut them.

Price penetration

A business will sell a product at a low price. This may be how they are differentiating their product. It is likely that this strategy will be used in the mass market with the aim to sell higher volumes to a greater proportion of the total market.

Loss leader

Sometimes, the price of a product is set so low that the business actually makes a loss on each sale. However, the hope is that by offering such good deals on some advertised products it will attract customers to visit the business and purchase other more profitable products at the same time.

Cost-plus

The cost of producing a product is calculated and then a percentage margin is added to establish a selling price. This is to ensure that the business makes a profit on each sale.

BlueWave Express have unveiled a new transport link between the seaside towns of AquaBay and OceanShores. They plan to run a direct service between the two major tourist areas. Their rivals provide a similar service that takes longer as they make many stops on the way. A news article said "BlueWave will now transport tourists seamlessly from one breathtaking town to another in half the time of anyone else."

Explain **one** benefit to BlueWave of using price skimming for its new route. [4]

BlueWave will be able to charge a high price because their service between the coastal towns is unique.[✓] Tourists will be happy to pay a higher price for a quicker route between AquaBay and OceanShores,[✓] because it will save them time as the new route only takes half the time of others.[✓] As a result BlueWave will experience increased revenues.[✓] / recover the costs of launching the new service more quickly.[✓]

The factors that influence pricing decisions

There are many factors that will influence which **pricing method** is best for a business to use.

Costs

A lower price can be charged when costs are kept to a minimum. But in order to make a profit, the business must have a good understanding of all of its costs.

Supply and availability of products

When a product is in short supply, a business can charge more for it as customers will be willing to pay more for a product that is harder to get.

Nature of the market

If demand for a product is growing, then the business is more able to utilise a high price strategy. In addition, if people in the target market have increasing disposable income, then the business will be able to charge more.

Product life cycle

In the early stages of a product's life (see **page 72**), a business can charge a higher price as demand for the product will be high. As it reaches the decline stage, the business may have to lower the price in order to prevent sales from falling.

Degree of competition

The more competitive a market, the more pressure there is to lower prices. If a business does not price competitively, they may find that they lose customers to rival businesses.

Location

If a business is located in an expensive area (that helps to further improve their brand image), they will be able to charge more for their products. Equally, by locating online, businesses can afford to charge lower prices as costs are minimised.

Quality of product

When a business has a higher quality product, they can charge more for it. Customers will be willing to pay more for a product that has unique functions, is more durable or performs better than rival products.

In an exam, you may be faced with a question that asks you to recommend which pricing strategy is best. In doing so you will have to look at the circumstances that the business is facing. Is their product unique? Is the market competitive? Do they sell a wide variety of products? How is their brand perceived? You need to use the case study to help make your recommendation. For example:

- If a business has a unique product that is differentiated from others in the market, then they could utilise price skimming.
- If a business is in a market with lots of competitors and the product is very similar to those being sold by other businesses, then they will likely need to use price penetration or competitor pricing.

THE MARKETING MIX: PRODUCT

Businesses need to understand that they have to develop new products in order to remain competitive, however they must also understand the risks involved. Businesses also need to consider how they will differentiate their product from others in a competitive market.

Product development

A business will develop new products in order to continue meeting the changing needs and wants of customers.

Benefit of developing new products

- A business' sales figures will hopefully grow. If a product is developed to extend the life or replace an existing, declining, product, sales figures won't fall.
- Widening the product range spreads the risk faced by the business of a single product failure.
- New products can enhance a business' image, particularly if they have had successful launches previously.

Risks of developing new products

- It can be expensive to develop new products as prototypes need to be made and tested. If the product is unsuccessful, the business can incur significant losses.
- Other businesses can closely copy new products which could quickly erode any competitive advantage gained.
- If the product does not meet customer expectations, it can have a negative impact on the business' reputation.

When developing a product, a business will need to consider:

- **Product design –** The design of the product incorporates the functionality, its features, and its appearance. If what is produced is unique then it will be differentiated from competitor products.

- **Image –** The new product should help to strengthen an already established brand image.

- **Needs of the target market –** The design must fit the needs of the specific group of customers who would buy the product.

Explain the importance of designing a product that meets the needs of the target market. [2]

Design must meet the needs of the customer so that they are satisfied with the product.[1] *This will mean that they will be more likely to return and purchase it again.*[1]

A business must **differentiate** its product to be successful in the market. This means making a product distinctive in some way when compared with rival products. There are two main ways that a business can differentiate its product, through having a **unique selling point** or by having a strong **brand image**.

Unique selling point

A unique selling point is a characteristic or feature of a product that makes it different from or significantly better than all other products in the market. A **USP** can also be gained from having unique packaging or outstanding customer service compared to rivals. Customers are likely to pay more for something that is unique.

Branding

Building a strong brand name will give a business a good reputation and make its products more desirable. This allows the business to increase the price. Customers will pay a premium so they can have or be associated with that branded product.

Having a strong brand benefits the business in the following ways:

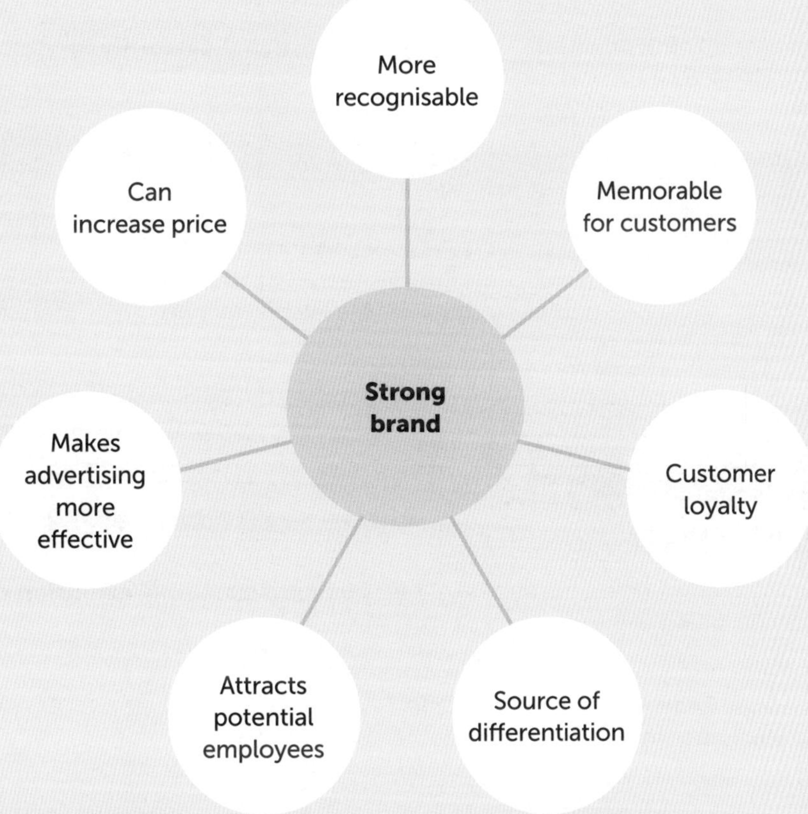

PRODUCT LIFE CYCLE

Every product has a life span. To ensure a business continues to be successful it needs to understand the life cycle of its products. If it believes that the sales of a product may soon start to fall, the business can take some actions to extend its life span.

The phases of the product life cycle

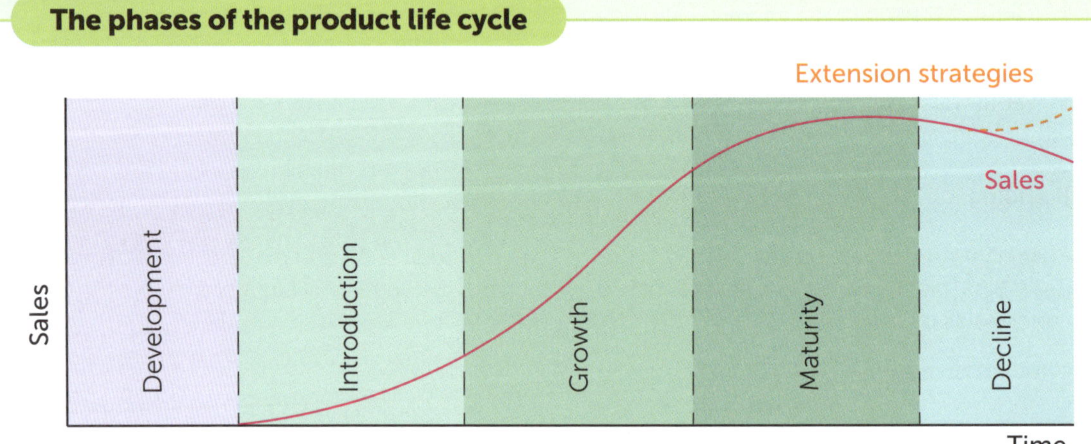

R&D	Introduction	Growth	Maturity	Decline
Research and development (**R&D**) is employed to come up with a marketable product. At pre-launch, no sales are made, but the business incurs lots of costs, so related cash flow is negative.	The product is launched onto the market. Sales start to increase. Cash flow is likely to remain negative as the business must heavily promote the product to develop awareness of it.	Sales will start to rise more rapidly after a successful launch as customers become more familiar with the product. As sales start to rise, cash flow starts to become positive.	Sales levels and cash flow are at their highest. However, growth in sales will start to slow down. The market may become saturated as more competitors enter the market.	Sales of the product decrease. This may be because the product is outdated. If this continues, the business may decide to withdraw the product.

Extension strategies

Before a business' product enters the decline phase, a business can use an **extension strategy** to extend the maturity phase of the life cycle.
It can do this by:

- Targeting a new market segment or new market
- Increasing the usage amongst existing customers
- Modifying the product
- Changing the image of the product
- Increasing promotion through advertising or price offers

In the exam you might have to suggest specific extension strategies that are relevant to the businesses that you read about in the case studies.

Aquatica Oasis, a once-thriving waterpark nestled in the heart of a bustling tourist destination, now faces a daunting challenge as its visitor numbers steadily decline. Founded 15 years ago with the promise of exhilarating aquatic adventures, the park has struggled to attract visitors in the face of evolving consumer tastes and expectations. Despite its scenic location and initial success, Aquatica Oasis has faltered due to a lack of innovation and investment in updating its rides and attractions. As newer, more innovative waterparks emerge, offering state-of-the-art experiences, Aquatica Oasis finds itself grappling with an outdated image and diminishing appeal to both locals and tourists alike.

Explain an extension strategy that Aquatica Oasis could utilise to extend its life cycle. [4]

Aquatica Oasis could develop new slides and rides for their waterpark.[1] *This is because they haven't updated them in 15 years.*[1] *Therefore, the new rides and experiences will help the waterpark to compete more effectively against the new parks that have emerged.*[1] *This will lead to more visitors purchasing tickets,*[1] *therefore preventing the business from falling deeper into decline.*[1]

Alternative strategies include new advertising campaigns or price reductions.

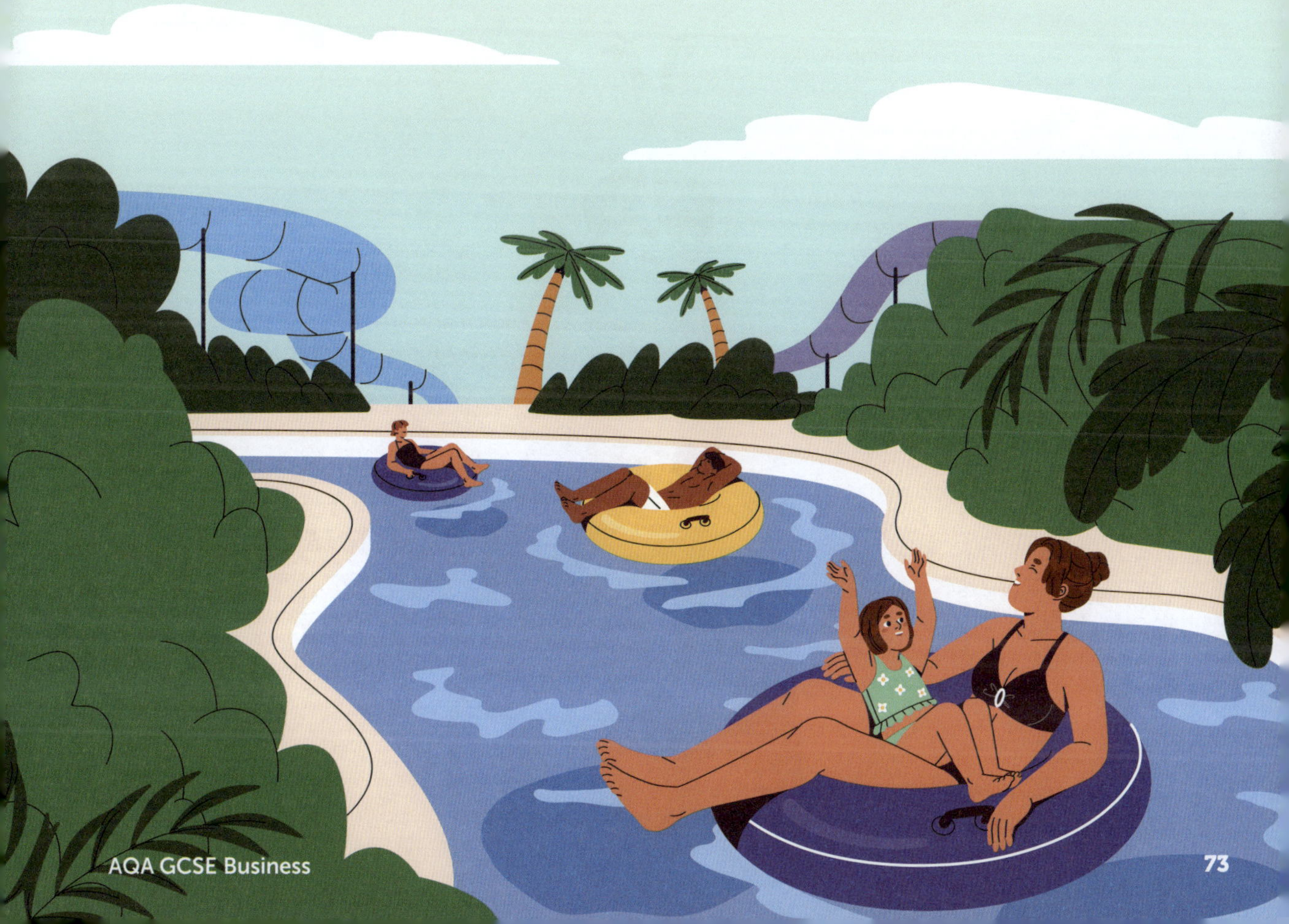

PRODUCT PORTFOLIO

When a business has a wide **product portfolio**, it should be well managed in order to improve the chances of being successful in the long term. The starting point is to analyse the products that a business has; one tool that businesses can use to achieve this is the **Boston matrix**.

Product range

A business may choose to have a wide product range for the following reasons:

- **To spread risk:** By having products in more than one market, a business is at less risk of failure should sales in one market start to decline.
- **To increase sales:** By having more products available to purchase, a business hopes that its sales will improve.

The Boston matrix

This matrix is a tool for analysing the effectiveness of a business' product range, by categorising them based on their market share and the rate of growth of the market. A business might broaden and balance their product portfolio with products in all categories.

This matrix is a tool for analysing the effectiveness of a business' product range, by categorising them based on their market share and the rate of growth of the market. A business might broaden and balance their product portfolio with products in all categories.

Cash cows

Cash cows are products that benefit from a large market share of a market that is not growing very fast. Therefore, it is likely that they will maintain this position, earning good income for the business, which can be used to support products in other categories.

Stars

Stars are products that experience a high market share of a high growth market. To maintain this strong position, businesses will need to back their product with advertising and promotion, otherwise competitors will try to steal market share away. The aim is that they eventually mature into cash cows.

Dogs

Businesses may decide to discontinue **dog** products. These are products which have a low market share of a low growth market. If the business chooses not to discontinue such products, then they may invest in them to make them more appealing to customers.

Question marks

A **question mark** is also called a 'Problem child' because businesses are not always sure what to do with these products. They have a low market share of a fast-growing market, so with investment, they have the potential to increase their market share and become a star.

A business will not always get rid of a dog product. For instance, a product may only have a low market share and the market may not be growing, but the market itself may be huge, therefore the dog product still generates a large amount of revenue for the business. An example is Cadbury's Fruit and Nut bars.

Explain why a business may want to have products in different categories of the Boston matrix. [2]

A business will want to have products in different categories so that they can broaden and balance their portfolio / continue to grow.[1] *The income generated from cash cows will be used to support products that are question marks so they can increase their market share of these products.*[1]

THE MARKETING MIX: PROMOTION

Promotion helps to create awareness of a business and its products. Its purpose is to instil the desire in a customer to want to purchase the product or to be associated with a brand by building a strong brand image.

Promotional methods

Advertising

Communication used to inform potential customers about the products and to persuade them to buy. It can take many forms: **newspapers**, **magazines**, **television**, **internet** and **billboards**.

Benefit: Can reach a large potential audience. Particularly effective for older generations.

Drawback: Can be expensive, especially if people ignore adverts, or watch TV on demand.

Sales promotion

Short-term incentives that a business uses in order to entice customers to purchase their goods. These include **point-of-sale displays**, **2 for 1 offers**, **free gifts**, **samples**, **coupons** and **competitions**.

Benefit: Customers feel they are getting a bargain.

Drawback: Profit margins will be reduced.

Social media

A lot of businesses will use social media apps in order to raise awareness and to communicate with their customers. This helps customers to engage with the business regularly.

Benefit: Can be a cost-effective way to promote the business, especially if a post goes viral.

Drawback: May not have the skills in the workforce to use this method effectively, and it may be ignored.

Public relations (PR)

Activities arranged in an attempt to pick up free media coverage of the business and its products. This could be done through **press releases**, **news articles**, **special events** or **celebrity endorsements**.

Benefit: A lot of the time, good PR can be free and it can reach a wide audience.

Drawback: The business has no control over the coverage and the activities may not always attract attention.

Sponsorship

A method of raising awareness of a business' brand name in return for financial support of events. Such events could be corporate, cultural, sporting or musical.

Benefit: Can provide a lot of brand exposure. Particularly effective when targeting events for specific market segments.

Drawback: If the event being sponsored gets bad publicity, the business' image may suffer by association.
It can also be expensive.

Finance available

Promotion can be expensive depending on the method. For instance, advertising on TV is much more expensive than using social media. Therefore, businesses with smaller promotional budgets may utilise a very different promotional mix compared to large multinational businesses that have access to greater finance and will likely utilise a more varied approach.

Competitor actions

If a business is in a market where a competitor is spending heavily on promotion, then the business is under pressure to use a similar promotional mix. If they don't, they could be at risk of losing customers.

The nature of the product or service

The promotional mix chosen should support the type of product that the business is wanting to portray. For instance, if they are aiming a product (such as oven chips or toilet tissue) at a mass market and are facing a lot of competitors selling similar products, then sales promotion may be appropriate. However, this wouldn't be so appropriate for a business that is selling a product that is deemed to be unique with a high-quality brand image.

The nature of the market

A small business operating in a small market will have a very different promotional mix to a large business that operates nationally or internationally. These businesses will be able to spend more on promotion in the hope that they will receive a larger amount of sales in return.

The target market

It's important a business knows who the target market is as this will also be a determining factor in terms of the promotional mix used. If aiming at an international market, then some form of digital promotion may be more appropriate. A small business operating in a local market will not undertake national promotion, such as TV advertising. Social media campaigns may appeal more to a young target market.

Explain **one** reason why a business may undertake promotion. [2]

Promotion may be used to change a product's image.[1] This is because a business can utilise advertising to demonstrate that the product is of high quality.[1]

Other reasons could include: to inform/remind customers of the product,[1] to create or increase sales,[1] to persuade the customers to buy the product.[1]

THE MARKETING MIX: PLACE

Place considers a business' location and the methods of distribution used. This determines how the product gets to the end consumer.

Methods of distribution

A **distribution channel** is the route that a product takes from where it is manufactured to where it is sold to the end consumer. This could be direct or could involve the use of a retailer or wholesaler.

Direct

Direct distribution is employed by businesses that sell their product directly to the customer. This allows the producer to engage in direct communication with the customer so they will know if there is a problem. This creates a better understanding of the changing needs of the customers so products can be adapted if needed. Many **e-commerce** businesses will sell directly to customers via their own website.

Retailers

Some manufacturers will sell their products to a **retailer**. This is a 'middle-man' who buys products from the producer in larger quantities and then sells them on for a higher price to the end consumer. The retailer is a more convenient place for a customer to buy from.

Wholesalers

A wholesaler is a large distribution company that will purchase products in bulk at a discounted rate from many different manufacturers and then sell them on to smaller retailers. This is a more efficient way for a manufacturing firm to distribute its products as it makes one large delivery instead of lots of smaller deliveries to all the retailers that stock its products.

Telesales

Some business will sell products over the telephone. A business may contact potential customers directly in an attempt to persuade them to buy their goods or services.

1. Explain **one** disadvantage to a business from conducting telesales. [2]

   Customers may find it annoying to be called by the business.[1] Therefore the business gets a negative reputation as a result.[1]

E-commerce and m-commerce

E-commerce is the buying and selling of goods and services over the internet. It also allows customers to make purchases at any time of day and at their own convenience, whilst allowing a business to reach a much wider target market. **M-commerce** is specifically the use of mobile devices to buy and sell goods.

Developments in the use of e-commerce have allowed businesses to sell their products and services to global website users. This has allowed businesses to enter foreign markets without the need for expensive physical locations. This keeps costs down so they can remain competitively priced.

Benefits

- Can reach new markets, including overseas.
- Can keep costs low by not having an expensive physical location.
- Can sell more products as websites aren't restricted by physical opening hours.
- More convenient for customers as they can order from home, leading to more sales.

Drawbacks

- Customers can easily make price comparisons, putting pressure on businesses to lower prices.
- Businesses will have to pay to distribute products over a greater distance, or pass this cost onto customers, making it more expensive.
- As customers cannot physically see the products, there may be high levels of returns.
- Business will have to make sure that their sites are secure so customers' personal details are not stolen.

Integrated nature of the marketing mix

For a business to be successful and obtain a competitive advantage, its needs to develop an integrated marketing mix. All the elements of the marketing mix will influence each other. If a business decides to produce a new, high-quality, luxury and innovative product utilising the latest technology, the product will influence other factors in the following ways:

Price: The product is likely to cost a lot to manufacture so the price will need to be set high to reflect this and provide a satisfactory margin.

Promotion: The promotion strategies used must be appropriate given the product is of a high quality and likely to be targeted at the premium market.

Place: To uphold the product's superior image it must be sold in suitable establishments that enhance this image. Distribution is not likely to be extensive in order to protect the luxury image.

2. Explain **one** way that promotion may impact on the price element of the marketing mix. [2]

A business may decide to conduct free promotion using regular posts on social media rather than using TV advertising.[1] So the overall costs to the business are lower.[1] This means that the business can charge a lower price for its product.[1] A promotional campaign may be trying to portray an image of luxury[1] and the price of the product needs to reflect this.[1] Consequently, the business may use a price skimming strategy.[1]

Bloomsbury Blossoms was established in the bustling streets of London's Covent Garden in the 1950s by the esteemed Turner family. The company has developed into a renowned upmarket chain of florists known for their exquisite arrangements and impeccable service. With humble beginnings rooted in a passion for floristry, the Turners infused their creations with a touch of elegance and sophistication, earning them a loyal customer base. Over the decades, their dedication to quality and attention to detail propelled Bloomsbury Blossoms to expand, with several branches now in key locations across the South East of England.

Now, the Turners are considering embracing technology to further extend their reach. Recognising changing consumer habits, they have set their sights on integrating e-commerce and m-commerce platforms into their business model in order to reach a broader audience, while maintaining the signature quality associated with the Bloomsbury Blossoms brand. Although committed to this venture, the Turners are determined to maintain their reputation of quality service that is associated with the business' heritage.

Despite their traditional stance as a high-priced florist renowned for sourcing only the finest flowers from select growers, Bloomsbury Blossoms recognises the importance of catering to a diverse customer base. With the potential move into e-commerce and m-commerce, the Turners acknowledge the need to adapt to shifting consumer preferences. In a bid to make their offerings more accessible to a wider audience, they are contemplating the introduction of a low-budget bouquet option. This initiative aligns with their commitment to inclusivity, ensuring that everyone can experience the beauty and joy that fresh flowers bring, regardless of budget constraints. While maintaining their commitment to quality remains paramount, the Turners understand that affordability is also a key consideration for many customers. By diversifying their product range to include budget-friendly options, Bloomsbury Blossoms aims to strike a balance between luxury and affordability.

The introduction of a low-budget bouquet option represents a bold step forward for Bloomsbury Blossoms, signalling their willingness to embrace change while staying true to their heritage. By embracing innovation and inclusivity, they seek to redefine the boundaries of luxury floristry and cement their position as leaders in the industry.

EXAMINATION PRACTICE

1. Which category within the Boston matrix represents a product with low market growth and a high market share? [1]

   A – Cash cow

   B – Dog

   C – Question mark

   D – Star

2. In which stage of the product life cycle is cash flow more likely to be at its highest? [1]

   A – Decline

   B – Development

   C – Growth

   D – Maturity

3. A market contains four businesses. Their sales data over the last two years is shown in Table 1.

	Year 1 Sales (£)	Year 2 Sales (£)
Business A	45,000	48,500
Business B	36,000	34,000
Business C	28,500	?
Business D	31,500	33,000
Total sales	**141,000**	**156,000**

Table 1

Using Table 1, calculate the change in the market share of Business C from Year 1 to Year 2. Show your answer to 2 decimal places. [4]

4. Explain **one** benefit to a business from having a strong brand. [2]

5. Explain **one** reason why a business may want to use sales promotion. [2]

6. Explain **one** reason why a business might use price skimming. [2]

For the following questions, you must refer to Case study 5 on the previous page.

7. Explain **one** way in which Bloomsbury Blossoms could segment the market. [4]

8. Explain **one** reason why Bloomsbury Blossoms must meet the needs of its customers. [4]

9. Analyse the reasons why Bloomsbury Blossoms will have conducted market research before deciding to expand. [6]

10. Analyse the reasons why Bloomsbury Blossoms should introduce e-commerce. [6]

11. Recommend whether Bloomsbury Blossoms should introduce a low-price range to its portfolio. [9]

SOURCES OF FINANCE

All businesses need finance whether they are just starting-up or whether they are well established. Businesses need finance for expansion, to invest in new products and technologies, and for paying for everyday expenses.

Sources of finance

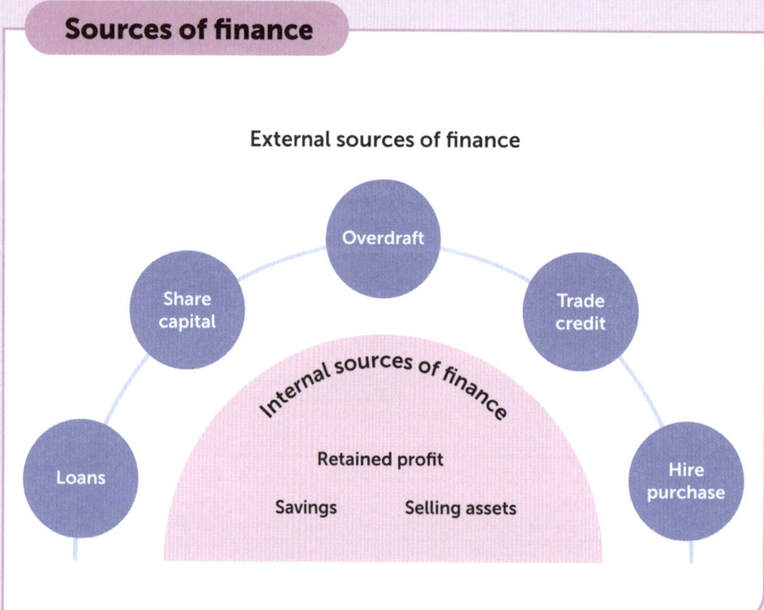

Which **one** of the following sources of finance would require interest payments?

A – Mortgage

B – Retained profit

C – Share capital

D – Trade credit [1]

A – Mortgage.[1]

Internal sources of finance

Retained profit

Retained profit that a business has generated and reserved can be reinvested. This source is cheaper than other methods and it allows the owners to maintain their control. However, once it is spent, the business will need to rebuild reserves before funding other projects. Whether it is suitable may be dependent on how much profit the business generates.

Selling assets

Assets are things that are already owed by a business, such as machinery, buildings or intellectual property. Selling assets is cheap as no repayments are necessary. The drawback of this option is that once sold, the business will not be able to use the assets. Whether **selling assets** is appropriate may be dependent on how much the assets are required.

Personal savings

The owners of sole traders and partnerships may choose to invest their own funds into the business. A benefit of this is that it does not need to be repaid, but it does mean that the owner won't have the funds available for anything else. If a business owner doesn't have any savings, they may also borrow finance from **friends and family**.

External sources of finance

Loans

A business may borrow money from a bank. They will make monthly **loan** repayments to the bank, which will include interest. A **mortgage** is a specific loan for purchasing property. Whether this is suitable may depend on how high the interest rate is and how much of a risk the bank thinks the business is.

Share capital

Share capital is finance raised by issuing or selling shares in a limited or public company. One benefit is that large amounts of funds can be sourced, while also keeping ongoing costs to a minimum as no repayments are made. However, depending on how many shares are given away, it could mean that the owners lose control.

Overdraft

An **overdraft** is an agreement with a bank that allows a business to spend more than they have in their bank account. This must eventually be repaid to the bank, usually with high interest. Businesses normally use this method to solve short-term cash flow issues.

Trade credit

Trade credit is offered when a business receives goods from a supplier but doesn't actually pay for them until after an agreed amount of time (e.g. 28 days).

Hire purchase

Hire purchase agreements operate like a loan and are usually used for the purchase of machinery, equipment and vehicles. The business would obtain the asset but would pay for it in instalments over time with (often high) interest added. The business would own the asset after the last instalment has been paid.

Government grants

A business can apply for money through a **government grant** if they meet certain criteria. This is often for setting up in areas of high unemployment. Grants are a cheap source of finance as the business will not usually need to pay it back, but the amount received may be limited.

How to suggest the most suitable source of finance:

In the exam, you may have to recommend which source of finance may be most suitable for the business that is presented in the case study. This may be influenced by a number of factors, including whether it's a new business or not. For example, a new business will have no retained profit to use, whereas an established business may.

Other factors such as the legal structure will impact the choice. Limited companies can issue shares to raise money whereas a sole trader or partnership cannot.

Look to see what circumstances the business in the case study is facing and use the information provided to help make your recommendation.

CASH FLOW

Cash flow is the amount of money flowing into and out of a business over a period of time. Having enough cash is critical to a business. Many businesses fail because they do not have sufficient cash to pay all their bills.

The importance of cash to a business

A business uses cash to pay for all its day-to-day expenses. This includes paying for its supplies and wages for its employees. Without their help, most businesses could not continue. Without supplies, the business could not produce its product or provide its service.

If a business does not have enough cash to pay for its bills when they are due, it is said to be **insolvent**. This will lead to the failure of the business.

1. Identify and explain **two** reasons why a business might run out of cash. [4]

1. *A business might experience seasonal sales.[1] This means that at certain times in the year they may have very little cash flowing into the business as they are not selling anything.[1]*

    There may be an unexpected rise in costs, for example the price of raw materials.[1] This would increase cash outflows, meaning a lower than expected closing balance every month.[1]

    Other reasons include: poor credit terms from suppliers; having too much cash tied up in stock that can't sell; unexpected changes in demand; overtrading (spending too much on expansion).

Difference between cash and profit

Cash is the amount of money that a business has available to pay for its day-to-day expenses. **Profit** is the difference between revenue and total costs. (See **pages 17 or 87**) A profitable business can still run out of cash. This is because a business records revenue as soon as a sale is made, but they may not receive actual payment immediately. In the interim period, large bills may become due, causing cash flow problems.

Interpreting cash flow forecasts

A **cash flow forecast** is a prediction of future cash inflows and outflows for a business. Below is an example:

£	Jan	Feb	Mar	Apr
Total receipts	110,000	90,000	70,000	80,000
Total payments	75,000	135,000	95,000	60,000
Net cash flow	35,000	(45,000)	(25,000)	20,000
Opening balance	25,000	60,000	15,000	(10,000)
Closing balance	60,000	15,000	(10,000)	10,000

A business will use a forecast to spot, in advance, when it is likely to have cash flow difficulties. Therefore, the business can take action to ensure that it does not run out of cash. In the example above, the business looks like it will have problems in March. Therefore, the business should take action to ensure that it doesn't encounter financial problems.

A short-term loan, overdraft, request for additional trade credit or re-scheduling payments may resolve the cash flow problem presented here.

Remember the following formulae. An exam question could ask you to fill in the blanks on a cash-flow forecast, but you won't have to create a complete forecast.

- Net cash flow = total receipts − total payments
- Closing balance = opening balance + net cash flow
- Opening balance is always the same as the previous month's closing balance

2. Look at the following extract from a cash flow forecast:

	January	February
Total cash inflows	13,425	13,700
Total cash outflows	14,650	13,750
Net cash flow	(1,225)	(50)
Opening balance	12,000	
Closing balance	10,775	

Calculate the closing balance for February. [2]

2. *February opening balance = 12,000 − 1225 = 10,775 or same as January closing balance*[1]

   February closing balance = 10,775 − 50 = £10,725[1]

IMPROVING CASH FLOW

When a business has identified that they may have cash flow issues in the future, it can plan a strategy to avoid the situation. There are various methods that a business can use to improve its cash flow.

Reducing cash outflows

A business can experience more positive cash flow if it reduces the amount that it pays out. This could be done by finding cheaper suppliers, undertaking less promotion or cutting overheads.

Arranging finance

A business could seek financial help from others in order to increase its receipts during periods of poor cash flow. This could be in the form of a bank **overdraft**.

Better stock management systems

A business could ensure that it does not have too much cash tied up in stock that doesn't sell, by ordering only the amount of materials that it needs, rather than holding stock just in case.

Rescheduling payments

This may allow a business to be able to receive cash in from customers before making the payment.

Better credit terms

A business could encourage its customers to pay cash up front rather than offering them **trade credit**. It could also ask for a longer period of trade credit from its suppliers.

Increasing cash inflow

A business can increase the inflow of cash to avoid cash flow problems. This can be done by seeking finance, by the owner putting more capital into the business or by introducing initiatives to sell more products.

Be careful not to simply suggest ways of improving sales that may actually worsen cash flow in the short term. For example, using expensive advertising to gain awareness may improve cash flow long term, but the business would have to pay for the advertising first, which may result in insolvency owing to a lack of cash to fund it.

FINANCIAL TERMS AND CALCULATIONS

To be able to accurately calculate **profit**, a business will need to know its **revenue** and its **total costs**. If a business can calculate these, then it can also carry out some analysis by looking at what profit it will make at different sales levels.

Revenue

Revenue is also referred to as **sales revenue** or **turnover**. It is the total amount of income made from selling a product or service. It is calculated by using the following formula:

Revenue = selling price × number of units sold

Fixed and variable costs

Fixed – **Fixed costs** are those that do not change in line with changes in output. An example would be advertising costs.

Variable costs – **Variable costs** are those that will change directly with changes in output. An example would be raw materials. The formula for total variable costs is:

Total variable costs = variable cost per unit × number of units sold

Remi makes homemade chocolates and sells them at local food fayres and in shops around her area. She has provided the following information:

- Average selling price of a box of chocolates: £5.50
- Fixed costs of running the business: £12,500
- Variable cost for each box of chocolates: £2.00

Calculate the profit made if Remi sells 5,000 boxes. [4]

Revenue = 5.50 × 5,000 = £27,500[1]

Total Variable cost = 2.00 × 5,000 = £10,000[1]

Total cost = FC + VC = 12,500 + 10,000 = 22,500[1]

Profit = Revenue – Total cost = 27,500 – 22,500 = £5,000[1]

Total costs

Total costs are all the costs added together that a business incurs in making a product or providing a service.

Total costs = fixed costs + variable costs

Profit

Profit is made when the revenue received exceeds the total costs. If a business has total costs that are greater than revenue it is called a **loss**.

Profit = Revenue – total costs

AVERAGE RATE OF RETURN

A business must often choose between different investment opportunities given the available finance. For instance, it could have to decide whether to purchase new machinery for its factory or to upgrade its delivery vans. Management will use the average rate of return to help decide which is best.

Investment projects that businesses undertake

Businesses will invest in new assets. They will use these assets to help produce goods and provide services. The main categories that businesses will invest in are:

Machinery

Buildings

Vehicles

Investment projects

Average rate of return

Before deciding which investment project to commit to, a business will calculate the **average rate of return** (**ARR**) of different investment projects in order to easily compare the financial merit of each option. ARR is a calculation that allows a business to work out the average yearly profit, as a percentage, on an investment.

Calculating average rate of return

To calculate the average rate of return (ARR) of a project, a business will use the following formula:

ARR = (Average return per annum ÷ initial sum invested) × 100

You may have to calculate the average return per annum first before applying the formula.

A quarrying company has the opportunity to invest in a new fleet of trucks. The cost of purchasing the vehicles is £36m. Over the next 6 years, it is anticipated they could generate an additional £54m of profit. Calculate the average rate of return if the quarrying company were to invest in the additional fleet. Show your working. [4]

Average return per annum = £54m ÷ 6 years[1] = £9m per year.[1]
Average rate of return = (£9m ÷ £36) × 100[1] = 25%[1]

The question in the exam may ask you to give your answer to 1 or 2 decimal places. If this is the case, make sure you follow the instructions so as not to lose marks.

Interpreting ARR

Average rate of return is a measure of profitability, so the higher the result the better. The quarrying company in the question on this page has the opportunity to invest in an additional fleet of trucks, and if it does so the predicted ARR is 25%. This means that for every £100 invested in the project, it will yield a yearly profit of £25.

If the quarrying company had a choice of investment projects to invest in, then it would, on financial grounds alone, select the investment with the highest percentage.

BREAK-EVEN

A firm will **break-even** when it sells enough products to generate sufficient revenue to cover its total costs. At the break-even point, revenue equals total costs, so the business makes no profit.

Break-even charts

Break even can also be shown diagrammatically with the use of a break-even chart. In this chart, a business will plot its costs and revenues at different output levels in order to find out the break-even level of output.

When constructing a break-even chart, revenue, total costs and fixed costs must each be plotted.

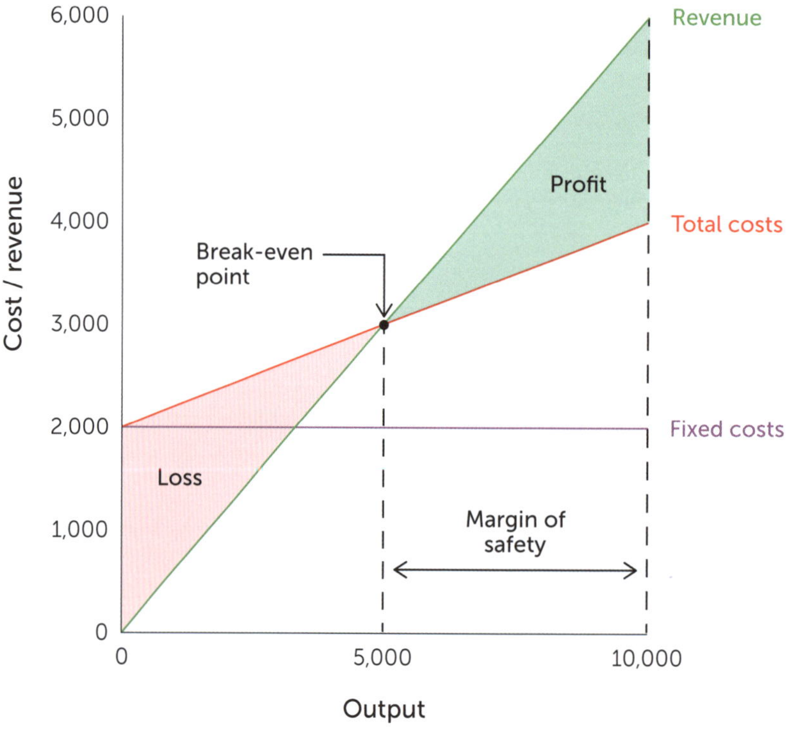

Fixed costs

Fixed costs are shown as a horizontal line on a break-even chart since fixed costs do not change with output. In the chart above, fixed costs are equal to £2,000.

Total costs *(variable + fixed)*

On a break-even chart, total costs will start from the same point as fixed costs. This is because a business that creates zero products will still have to pay the fixed costs, even if they will have no variable costs at that point.

Revenue

A business that sells zero products will receive no revenue. For this reason, the revenue line on a break-even chart starts at (0,0).

Businesses can use a break-even chart to find out the following information:

Break-even point

This is also known as the **break-even level of output**. As you can see in the chart opposite, this particular business needs to sell 5,000 products in order to receive enough revenue to cover its total costs. At this point, profit would be £0; neither a profit nor a loss is made.

Profit (loss)

Beyond the break-even point, revenue exceeds total costs. Therefore, the business is making a profit at any output level above 5,000. Below the break-even level of output, total costs are greater than revenue, so the business is making a loss.

Margin of safety

The **margin of safety** is the difference between the actual output of a business and the break-even level of output. If the business in the chart opposite is producing 10,000 units, then the margin of safety will be 5,000 units (10,000 – 5,000). This means that sales can drop by 5,000 units before the business becomes unprofitable.

Usefulness of break-even

Advantages and disadvantages of break-even

Break even analysis is particularly useful for new start-up businesses as it will allow them to see if their business is viable. This is because they will know how many products they need to sell to cover their costs and can then decide whether that is an achievable amount.

Break-even is used for 'what-if' analysis. A business can change the variables such as the selling price and variable cost per unit, to see what impact that has on the level of break even. This will also tell decision makers what might happen to profit levels, so they can create a strategy related to price, production levels and costs.

Identify and explain **two** disadvantages to a business of using break-even analysis. [4]

Break-even assumes all products are sold.[1] In reality, some products will be made but left unsold, which would mean a higher break-even point than if they had been sold.[1]

Variable cost per unit are assumed to remain the same.[1] This is not usually the case because a business buying in bulk from a supplier will often receive a discount, which would make the break-even point lower.[1]

Prices of raw materials may also change over time as new stock is ordered[1] which could alter the break-even point.[1]

Break-even assumes that every product is sold at the same price point.[1] An increase in sales price would create a lower break-even point / could cause lower sales.[1]

ANALYSING THE FINANCIAL PERFORMANCE OF A BUSINESS

There are different measures that a business may use in order to assess its financial performance. These include looking at the business' income statement and statement of financial position. These statements can be used to assess profitability.

Purpose of financial statements

Businesses create financial statements for the following reasons:
- To assess business performance.
- To comply with legislation.
- To help investors and stakeholders make decisions.
- To help managers to make decisions about the best course of action to take.

Income statements

An **income statement** is a financial document that details a company's revenues, costs and profits (or losses) over a specific period.

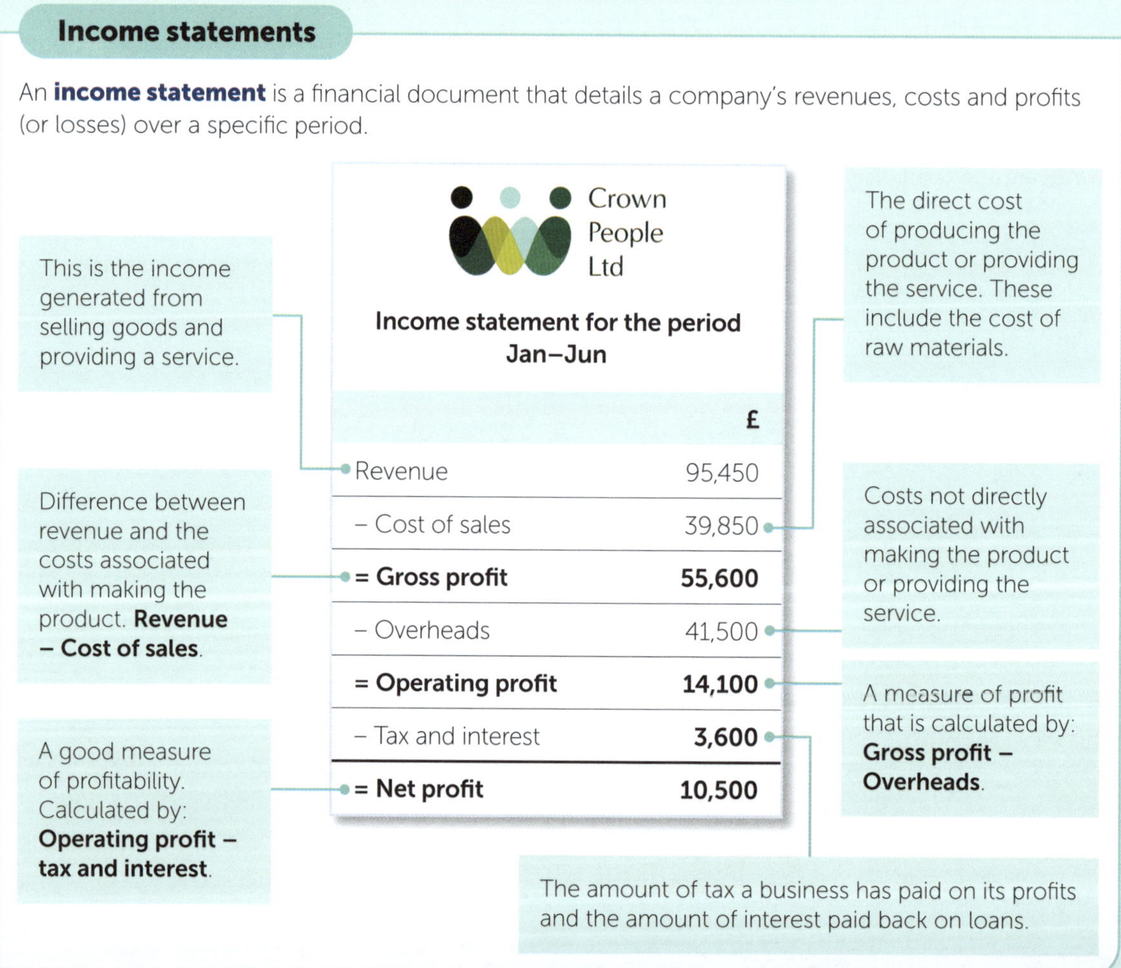

This is the income generated from selling goods and providing a service.

Difference between revenue and the costs associated with making the product. **Revenue – Cost of sales**.

A good measure of profitability. Calculated by: **Operating profit – tax and interest**.

The direct cost of producing the product or providing the service. These include the cost of raw materials.

Costs not directly associated with making the product or providing the service.

A measure of profit that is calculated by: **Gross profit – Overheads**.

The amount of tax a business has paid on its profits and the amount of interest paid back on loans.

Statement of financial position

A **statement of financial position** is a document that details the assets and liabilities of a business at the date of the document. It is a snapshot in time. It shows where a business' finances have come from and where they have been spent.

Assets that a business keeps for more than a year. These include items such as vehicles, machinery and buildings.

The short-term debts of the business. These debts must be paid back in the next twelve months.

This shows the value of the business. It is calculated as: **Assets – liabilities**

The business' liquid assets (assets that are cash or will be turned into cash within a year) including inventories and cash.

Long-term debts of the business, that will be paid back over many years. These include bank loans.

This figure will always equal the net assets figure. It is the value of the money that belongs to the shareholders.

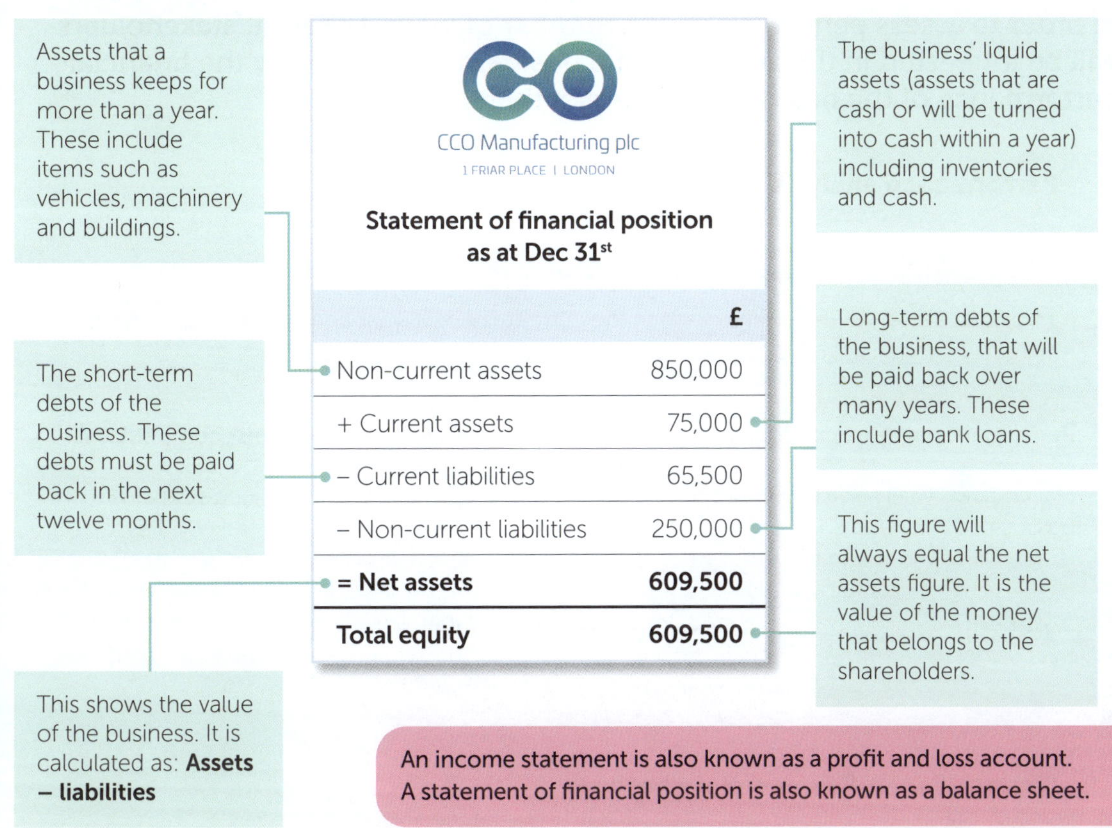

An income statement is also known as a profit and loss account. A statement of financial position is also known as a balance sheet.

Below is an extract from a business' statement of financial position:

	£
Non-current assets	880,000
Inventories	140,000
Cash	68,000
Total assets	1,088,000

Since the statement was produced, inventories have increased in value by 20%. The value of all other assets has stayed the same. Calculate the new total assets figure. Show your working. [4]

Increase in inventories value = 140,000 × 1.2[1] = £168,000[1]

New total assets = 880,000 + 168,000 + 68,000[1] = £1,116,000[1]

INTERPRETING THE FINANCIAL STATEMENTS

A business will use the income statement and statement of financial position in order to assess performance in a number of ways. Different stakeholders will be interested in the accounts of a business to assess how the financial performance of the business will impact them.

Performance analysis

Current performance

A business will look at the profits made in the current financial year and see how they compare to targets that they will have set themselves.

Performance against previous years

Stakeholders will look to compare how the business has done in comparison to previous years to see if any trends can be identified or to see if the business has shown growth. They will look to see if sales have increased. Has profitability improved? Is the business in a stronger financial position?

Performance against competitors

Profitability will be judged against rivals in the same market. Sales comparisons will also be made to see if the same trends are widespread, or if the business experienced more rapid growth in sales compared to others.

Financial accounts and stakeholders

Stakeholder	Why they are interested and how accounts help
Owners / shareholders	Shareholders will want to see higher profits so that they can receive increased dividends. If the business is perceived to be performing well financially, then they will also hope to see an increase in their share price.
Employees	Employees will want job security and increased wages. The statement of financial position will help to show the financial stability of the business as it shows how much they owe to others (liabilities) and the assets that the business has. If the business is experiencing improved sales and rising profits, then they may be able to seek an increase in pay.
Suppliers	Suppliers will want to see that the business is financially secure so that it can continue to pay them on time and so that they continue to receive orders.
Bank / potential investors	When deciding whether to provide finance, potential investors will assess the financial strength of the business.

The **gross profit margin** is a measure of how profitable a business is at making and selling its goods or services. The margin shows the profit as a percentage of revenue. It is calculated by:

Gross profit margin = (Gross profit ÷ revenue) × 100

The **net profit margin** is a test of the overall profitability of a business as it considers all the expenses of the business. The formula for net profit margin is:

Net profit margin = (Net profit ÷ revenue) × 100

You will not be given these formula in an exam, so you will need to remember them.

Income statement for the period Jan–Dec

	£
Revenue	95,450
– Cost of sales	39,850
= Gross profit	55,600
– Overheads	41,500
= Operating profit	14,100
– Tax and interest	3,500
= Net profit	10,600

Gross profit margin
(55,600 ÷ 95,450) × 100 = 58.25%

Net profit margin
(10,600 ÷ 95,450) × 100 = 11.11%

In the example above, the net profit margin is 11.11%, this means that for every £1 of revenue received, 11.11p of it is net profit.

Dylan runs a football coaching business. His weekly revenue from coaching sessions is £2,500. His cost of sales is £575. Other expenses are £425.

Calculate the gross profit margin for his coaching business. [2]

Gross profit = 2,500 – 575 = £1,925[1]

Gross profit margin = (1,925 ÷ 2,500) × 100 = 77%[1]

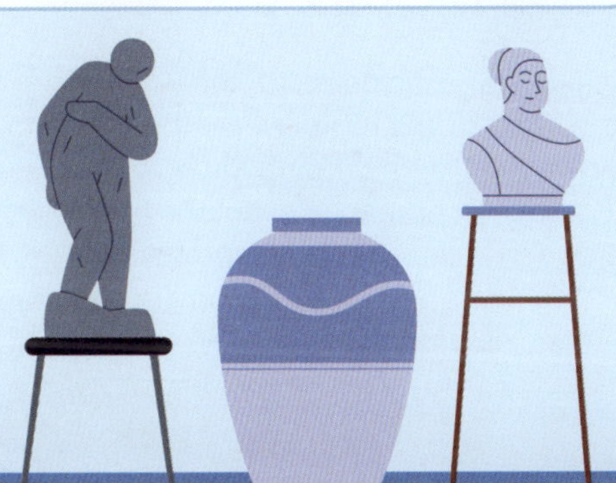

As a leading online television entertainment company, StreamFlix PLC has revolutionised the way audiences consume their favourite movies, TV series, and sports content. Operating on a subscription-based model, StreamFlix offers subscribers access to a vast library of the latest blockbuster releases and television shows. Beyond traditional entertainment offerings, StreamFlix distinguishes itself with a excellent sports coverage, showcasing a diverse range of live events from around the globe, catering to all the interests of its subscribers.

With a strategy to continue expanding its sports portfolio, StreamFlix is contemplating a bid for the rights to broadcast the next international women's football tournament. However, the substantial cost of £500 million for global rights presents a formidable financial challenge. To finance this ambitious project, StreamFlix must consider options such as borrowing capital or issuing additional shares. The decision to pursue this investment hinges on its potential to enhance the platform's value proposition and attract a broader audience, thereby increasing subscription revenues over the longer term.

Income Statement for StreamFlix for past and current years:

Last year	£m
Revenue	4,708
Cost of sales	3,808
Gross profit	900
Overheads	767
Operating profit	133
Tax and interest	30
Net profit	103

Current year	£m
Revenue	5,650
Cost of sales	4,232
Gross profit	1,418
Overheads	867
Operating profit	551
Tax and interest	123
Net profit	

Financial planning is critical for StreamFlix as it evaluates the feasibility of bidding for the women's football tournament rights. They anticipate that by having the rights to the tournament, they will also be able to significantly increase their revenue from advertising as well as increasing the number of subscribers. Before committing to such a significant investment, the company's directors recognise the importance of conducting a break-even analysis. By determining the additional number of subscribers needed to cover the increased cost of broadcasting the tournament, StreamFlix can make informed decisions about the potential return on investment and assess the project's financial viability. This strategic approach ensures that StreamFlix remains financially prudent while pursuing growth opportunities that align with its long-term objectives.

EXAMINATION PRACTICE

1. Which **one** of the following would be classed as a cash outflow for a business? [1]
   A – Investment from the sale of shares
   B – Rent received
   C – Repayments on a bank loan
   D – Sales revenue

2. Which **one** of the following is an internal source of finance? [1]
   A – Hire purchase
   B – Mortgage
   C – Sale of assets
   D – Share issue

3. A business sells products for £12.00. Its fixed costs are £3,200 a month, and the variable cost per unit is £4.50. Calculate the monthly profit if the business sells 600 products a month. [4]

4. Explain **one** way in which a business can improve its cash flow position. [2]

5. Explain **one** benefit to a business from using trade credit. [2]

For the following questions, you must refer to Case study 6 on the previous page.

6. Using the information in the income statement, calculate StreamFlix's net profit margin for the current year. Give your answer to **one** decimal place. [4]

7. StreamFlix expects to make an additional £120m profit spread over the next three years from obtaining the rights to the tournament. Using the case study, calculate the ARR if StreamFlix purchases the broadcasting rights. State the formula for ARR and show your workings. [5]

8. Explain **one** reason why StreamFlix should calculate the number of extra subscribers it will need to break-even. [4]

9. Analyse the reasons why the suppliers of the TV rights to the women's football tournament might be interested in the financial accounts of StreamFlix. [6]

10. Analyse the performance of StreamFlix over the past 12 months using the information contained in the income statements for the past and current year. [6]

11. StreamFlix may bid for the rights to broadcast the next women's international football tournament. It is considering two options to fund this:
    - Taking out a bank loan
    - Issuing new shares

    Evaluate which of these two options would be the most suitable option for SteamFlix to use. [12]

EXAMINATION PRACTICE ANSWERS

1. B – Merger. [1]

2. D – Tertiary. [1]

3. Raw materials.[1] Packaging.[1] Wages (when based on what they produce).[1] Energy used in the production process.[1] Commission paid to salespeople.[1] [2]

4. A business may be obliged to use more renewable energy sources / packaging,[1] which could increase costs for the business.[1] [2]

5. In order to help obtain finance from the bank.[1] This is because the entrepreneur can show that they have forecast income and costs showing that they are likely to get paid back.[1] / To plan for many potential eventualities,[1] thereby reducing risk of economic change / negative impacts on the business.[1] / To set objectives[1] which can be shared with employees and other stakeholders to provide direction and motivation.[1] / To detail how each function of a business should be organised[1] so that they each get the resources necessary to fulfil their role in the organisation effectively. [2]

6. A business could set itself a target for market share,[1] which it can then measure itself against as to how much of the market it controls and compare that with the target it set itself.[1] / Profit is a common objective[1] which can be easily measured against objectives and previous periods.[1] / Customer satisfaction targets[1] can be set and measured through surveys and ratings which can be compared against the target as well as competitors or historic scores.[1] [2]

7. An employee may be unhappy with the level of pay,[1] and as a result, they may go on strike meaning less work gets done.[1] / A member of the community[1] may not be happy with the levels of noise / pollution / traffic caused by a business and campaign against it.[1] / The government[1] may introduce new taxes / laws / minimum wages / regulations that impact the costs / import or exporting / ease of business.[1] / Suppliers[1] may change their terms / production levels / quality which could impact a business without alternatives.[1] / Customers[1] may not be happy with the quality or terms of service and may complain publicly (e.g. on social media).[1] [2]

8. Employees in the Chinese factory.[1] Owners / shareholders of the Chinese factory.[1] Shareholders of Landmark plc.[1] Board of Directors of Landmark plc.[1] [2]

9. Total variable costs = 5000 cars × 2500 = £12,500,000[1]; Total Costs = 3,750,000 + 12,500,000 = £16,250,000[1]; Total Revenue = 5000 × 9995 = £49,975,000[1]; Profit = 49,975,000 − 16,250,000 = £33,725,000[1] [4]

10. **This question should be marked in accordance with the levels-based mark scheme on page 105.**
    Landmark will benefit from technical economies of scale.[✔] This is because as they grow, they can afford more advanced technology to use in their production of cars.[✔] As a result, they will be able to produce more cars in the same amount of time. (they can produce cars in 20% less time).[✔] This will lead to lower average cost for each car made.[✔]
    Landmark could benefit from purchasing economies of scale.[✔] This is because as a market leader, they will be buying huge amounts of car parts.[✔] As a result of buying in bulk they will receive a greater discount.[✔] This will enable them to have lower average costs per car[✔] which would allow the car manufacturer to lower the price of the car[✔] which would be more attractive to potential customers.[✔] [4]

11. **This question should be marked in accordance with the levels-based mark scheme on page 105.**
    One drawback is that Landmark will be at risk of being taken over by other car manufacturers.[✔] This is because anyone could purchase shares in the car manufacturer.[✔] This means that should a rival car manufacturer want to benefit from the Landmark Boost, they could control it by purchasing a majority of the business' shares.[✔] As a result, the directors of the car manufacturer will likely lose their roles.[✔] This may mean the advantages that the business had gained in terms of efficient car production may disappear as the companies merge.[✔] This is because the leaders who had that expertise and knowledge may no longer be working in the business.[✔] These managerial concerns may cause diseconomies of scale[✔] and Landmark may no longer be able to produce the Boost as cheaply as they did,[✔] causing the new directors to have to increase the price from £9,995 for the hatchback.[✔] [6]

12. **This question should be marked in accordance with the levels-based mark scheme on page 105.**
    One factor could be close proximity to good transport links.[✔] To make the Boost hatchbacks, Landmark will require a large amount of metal parts, doors, gear sticks and seats which will all need to be delivered to the factory.[✔] Once manufactured, Landmark will need to deliver the cars to showrooms across the country. By having good access to transport links, it helps to keep delivery systems more efficient (particularly as they are wanting to deliver overseas)[✔] which therefore helps to keep costs low.[✔] This helps the car manufacturer to be able to keep the price of the Boost at a competitively priced £9,995.[✔] This therefore means they can target the mass market with their car,[✔] which will help to maximise sales of their vehicles.[✔]
    Another factor could be proximity to cheap labour.[✔] Landmark will require a lot of staff to build cars and manage production,[✔] so they may locate their factory premises close to a heavily populated area[✔] with the right skills, levels of employment and low labour costs.[✔] This will help to keep the cost of production to a minimum,[✔] which will help to keep the overall price of the Boost as it is.[✔] This will help Landmark to be more competitive with other manufacturers.[✔] [6]

13. **This question should be marked in accordance with the levels-based mark scheme on page 106.**

I recommend that the car manufacturer should pursue a takeover in order to grow.[✔] This is because it can be a very quick way for the car company to increase its sales.[✔] They are looking to purchase a Chinese car manufacturing rival,[✔] meaning that once the takeover has gone through, they will then own that business.[✔] As a result, the sales of the Chinese car manufacturer will now be theirs,[✔] which could potentially increase their profits dramatically.[✔]

However, purchasing the Chinese car manufacturer will cost Landmark a lot of money,[✔] as they will have to persuade the Chinese firm's shareholders to part with their shares.[✔] This will mean that they will have to raise a large amount of finance,[✔] which may be very costly.[✔] This could result in the Landmark having to increase its price of the existing cars such as the Boost, in order to maintain profit levels.[✔] This may mean that they lose their value in the car market,[✔] which could lead to sales decreasing for their existing cars,[✔] eroding any potential increase in profit.[✔]

Overall, I think that pursuing a takeover is better than growing by opening more manufacturing bases in the UK, mainly because their sales have remained stagnant.[✔] By buying another firm, not only do they gain the sales of the Chinese car manufacturer, but they also get a quick foothold into a foreign market,[✔] which could potentially lead to a huge increase in sales.[✔] Building more manufacturing bases in the UK is just going to flood the UK market with more Boosts which may not sell so although there is more risk,[✔] acquiring the Chinese car manufacturer is the best option. However, this is dependent on the price they must pay and whether Landmark can gain access to sufficient funds to make it happen.[✔]   [9]

Section 3.2   Influences on business

1. D – May not get noticed online amongst higher competition.   [1]

2. A – Businesses will have a greater pool of potential candidates to recruit from.   [1]

3. One method with linked explanation. A business can set up a profile on popular social media[1] sites and post messages which the customers can respond to.[1] Online chat(bots)[1] can be used to provide support to website users.[1] Mobile apps[1] can help to provide information, alerts or more convenient purchasing.[1] Websites[1] can detail product information and provide an online shop window. [1] Video calls [1] can be used to provide remote support to customer queries or to demonstrate a digital product.[1] Blogs and newsletters [1] can be used to provide regular updates or to promote thought leadership.[1]   [2]

4. One method with linked explanation. Using locally sourced raw materials[1] helps to reduce a business' carbon footprint as the materials won't need to be transported very far.[1] Renewable energy[1] could be used to power factories or offices. [1] Electric vehicles[1] could be used as part of a company delivery fleet.[1] All waste can be recycled [1] to reduce landfill.[1] Products can use more recycled materials / packaging[1] to reduce the demand for / reliance on raw materials.[1] Production methods could use fewer harmful chemicals / reduce harmful waste[1] which would reduce the risk of contamination / leakage into the environment / pollution.[1]   [2]

5. One method with linked explanation. One benefit is that a business may now have access to cheaper materials from abroad[1] which allows them to reduce their costs / pass on savings to the consumer in the form of lower prices.[1] Access to a much larger market[1] so growth can increase rapidly.[1] Inward investment[1] can come from a wider pool internationally.[1]   [2]

6. One risk identified with linked explanation. One risk is that the business receives bad publicity[1] which could ruin the reputation of the business and therefore they see a decline in sales.[1] Competition may rapidly increase / launch a new and improved product[1] which would cause customers to change loyalties, reducing sales.[1] A key supplier may be lost[1] meaning that more expensive / cheaper quality alternatives will need to be sourced affecting product costs or quality. [1] Economic change / legislation[1] may reduce consumer spending / increase minimum wages (costs).[1] Key employees may leave[1] increasing costs in recruitment and training / reducing productivity.[1]   [2]

7. Two points with linked explanations. Health and safety laws may require changes to the workplace to make it safer for employees[1] which would come at a cost to the business.[1] Compliance with all legislation[1] may increase motivation amongst workers as the business is seen as a good employer / employees will be more inclined to stay with the business.[1] Employment law may increase the national wage[1] causing an increase in wage costs for businesses.[1] Businesses may need to employ administration staff / consultants[1] at extra cost to deal with the legislation / check requirements are met.[1] [4]

8. **This question should be marked in accordance with the levels-based mark scheme on page 105.**
One impact is that there will be pressure to sell their wraps and burritos at low prices to compete with other restaurants.[✔] This is because there will be many other restaurants selling similar fast food options at competitive prices.[✔] As a result, there is a danger that cash flow is not as high as it might have been.[✔] Therefore, Wrap Nation may struggle to meet the repayments on the debt that it has accrued.[✔]   [4]

9. **This question should be marked in accordance with the levels-based mark scheme on page 105.**
In the UK, Wrap Nation restaurants import ingredients from Europe.[✔] If the Pound were to increase in value it would make these ingredients cheaper against the Euro.[✔] As a result, the fast food chain's costs would decrease,[✔] which would allow them to lower the price of their wraps and burritos.[✔] Making them more competitive compared to rivals, Bite.[✔] / increase profits for the company[✔] allowing them to pay off their debt more quickly.[✔]   [4]

10. **This question should be marked in accordance with the levels-based mark scheme on page 105.**

One benefit is that it has allowed Wrap Nation to introduce an app.[✔] This is more convenient for customers as they can order their food through the app and it will be ready on arrival.[✔] This will increase customer satisfaction with the service that they receive.[✔] As a result it will make customers more likely to return to Wrap Nation.[✔] This will result in an increase in sales of wraps and burritos,[✔] which would potentially lead to increased profits.[✔]

[6]

11. **This question should be marked in accordance with the levels-based mark scheme on page 105.**

Interest rates apply to the cost of borrowing.[✔] The payments on the debt owed by Wrap Nation would increase.[✔] Fixed costs will rise sharply.[✔] Wrap Nation currently have a large amount of loans.[✔] This would vastly reduce cash flow for the fast food chain.[✔] If the rise was significant, it may mean that they don't have enough inflow of cash from selling wraps and burritos in order to meet the necessary repayments.[✔] As a result, they may have to sell some of their restaurants to raise enough cash for the repayments.[✔]

[6]

12. **This question should be marked in accordance with the levels-based mark scheme on page 106.**

One reason why Wrap Nation should change its packaging is because they will gain reputational benefits as a result.[✔] This is because they should be using less plastic in their packaging of their wraps and burritos.[✔] As a result, there will be less plastic that is potentially littered or thrown into landfill.[✔] Therefore, the fast food chain will reduce their impact on the eco-systems in which they operate.[✔] Consequently, ethically minded customers may be more likely to eat at the restaurants.[✔] Therefore, the revenue and potential profits earned by the fast food chain may increase.[✔]

However, changing from plastic packaging to a recyclable material may be more expensive.[✔] This would lead to increased variable costs,[✔] which will increase the cost of providing each wrap or burrito.[✔] As a result, the fast food chain may need to pass this increased cost onto consumers in the form of higher prices.[✔] This may mean that rivals such as Bite, are able to sell their food at a comparatively lower price, [✔] which will attract customers away from Wrap Nation.[✔] This would mean that the restaurant chain would experience a lower share of the fast food market.[✔]

In conclusion, whether they decide to change their packaging to recyclable materials depends on the ethical consciousness of its customers.[✔] If a lot of customers react angrily to the article that highlighted their use of plastics and the damage it was causing the eco-systems around them, then they would have little choice but to change.[✔] If customers are more concerned about price, then keeping costs low in the competitive fast food market by using cheaper packaging may be the best course of action.[✔]

[9]

Section 3.3   Business operations

1. B – Giving good customer service.

[1]

2. B – Fewer defective products.

[1]

3. Businesses can now use social media to gain feedback from customers[1] which allows a business to alter the product or process according to what customers have said.[1] E-commerce enables customers to browse or shop at their leisure / 24–7 / in the comfort of their home[1] which increases the sales window / removes any awkward sales pressure / means that those unable to get to physical shops can make purchases, increasing sales.[1] Websites[1] can be used to provide more detailed product information / videos to help inform the shopper and keep in touch with brand developments, improving loyalty and sales.[1]

[2]

4. One benefit is that a business can reduce physical waste[1] which will help the business to reduce costs.[1] Employee time is optimised / wasted time is reduced[1] which improves productivity and reduces the overall cost of output per unit.[1]

[2]

5. The business will be able to gain supplies at the best possible price[1] therefore they can lower the price charged to customers, increasing sales.[1] Supplies will be trusted to be delivered on time / as ordered[1] which reduces any problems with production and associated costs / prevents delays in getting goods to the customer, affecting customer service / reputation.[1] Waste is reduced[1] which can lower costs / improve output / production times.[1]

[2]

6. **This question should be marked in accordance with the levels-based mark scheme on page 105.**

One drawback is that there is the potential that the production of sweets may have to stop[✔] which would happen if the delivery of the sugar supplies was delayed for some reason.[✔] This would mean that the confectionery manufacturer would not have any supplies to use on the production line because with JIT no stock is held.[✔] As a result, the sweets will be delayed in arriving at the shops meaning that customers may choose something else.[✔]

It becomes more difficult to benefit from bulk discounts / economies of scale[✔] when using JIT stock control because the orders of SugarX would be generally smaller and more frequent.[✔] This increases the unit cost of each sweet / pack of sweets[✔] which would have a knock-on impact on either profits or increased prices.[✔] Increased prices may cause customers to find a cheaper alternative sweet.[✔]

[4]

7. **This question should be marked in accordance with the levels-based mark scheme on page 105.**

Sweet Delights could provide excellent knowledge of / product information on the sweets.[✔] This is because SweetDelights Ltd sells to retailers / wholesalers who then sell the sweets onto the end consumer.[✔] As a result, a retailer will need to know about the ingredients used in the sweets and information about their nutritional value / allergies,[✔] as they will need to pass this information onto the person that consumes the sweets.[✔]

[4]

8. **This question should be marked in accordance with the levels-based mark scheme on page 105.**

Flow production allows SweetDelights to mass produce their sweets.[✔] As they are manufacturing such large quantities of the confectionery, they can buy the ingredients (such as SugarX) in large quantities.[✔] As a result, the supplier is more likely to offer a discount for buying the sugar in bulk / large quantities over time.[✔] This will mean that the average cost of producing a bag of sweets is reduced. [✔] This will allow the business to sell the sweets to retailers for a lower price / increase the profit per bag,[✔] resulting in the manufacturer becoming more competitive against other confectionery firms / increasing overall profits.[✔]

The machinery / robotics necessary for mass production involve a very high initial cost.[✔] These will then need regular servicing and maintenance by skilled engineers,[✔] who may need to be additionally employed,[✔] increasing the overhead costs.[✔] Without additional maintenance engineers, the production line may break down,[✔] causing all production to stop.[✔] Sweet Delights may benefit from reduced payroll as the production line may replace a lot of manual labour roles. [✔] Those remaining on the production line may become more specialist[✔] at their individual jobs which would boost productivity,[✔] but there is a risk that the repetition will demotivate them,[✔] lowering productivity.[✔]   [6]

9. **This question should be marked in accordance with the levels-based mark scheme on page 105.**

Quality is important as the confectionery firm has built up a reputation for manufacturing high quality sweets.[✔] Therefore, the end consumers will expect the sweets to continue to be of a high quality moving forward.[✔] This will be a source of differentiation for the sweet manufacturer[✔] and therefore means that they can charge a higher price for a bag of sweets.[✔] This is because retailers will pay a higher amount in order to stock the sweets.[✔] They will pay this because they know that the end consumer will be more likely to visit them if they have the sweets in stock.[✔]   [6]

10. **This question should be marked in accordance with the levels-based mark scheme on page 106.**

The advantage of switching to Supplier B is that it is offering SugarX at a lower price.[✔] Therefore, the cost of ingredients may be lower,[✔] variable costs are reduced.[✔] As a result, the average cost of producing each bag of sweets will be lower.[✔] This will allow SweetDelights to lower the price to its customers,[✔] the retail outlets where the bags of sweets are sold.[✔] The hope is that this would result in sales increasing[✔] which would increase the revenue[✔] and therefore potentially the profit of the confectionery firm.[✔]

However, SweetDelights has built up a loyal and reliable relationship with its current supplier.[✔] This may be of benefit to SweetDelights, particularly as they are utilising a system of just in time (JIT) stock control currently.[✔] They need to trust that deliveries of SugarX will be on time, otherwise production of the sweets will be disrupted.[✔] Supplier B is a new company and their reliability is untested.[✔] This may be too much of a risk for SweetDelights to take,[✔] as it could have negative consequences on their reputation if manufacturing is delayed.[✔]

In conclusion I believe that they should stick with their existing supplier rather than changing to Supplier B.[✔] This is because the confectionery firm has worked hard to build up its reputation and reliable delivery is a crucial part of that process, particularly because of their use of JIT.[✔] However, my decision depends on whether their current supplier can continue to deliver SugarX at reasonable prices.[✔] If they become too expensive then Supplier B may just be worth the risk.[✔]   [9]

Section 3.4 Human resources

1. C – Qualifications that are necessary to carry out the job.   [1]

2. B – The number of people that a line manager is directly responsible for.   [1]

3. A structure allows a business to organise its employees.[1] This will allow the employees to know how they fit into the organisation and who their line manager is should they need help.[1] / Employees can get a better sense of who does each job role in a business[1] so they can understand how they interconnect / where they sit within the organisation / see where responsibilities lie / understand the chain of communication.[1]   [2]

4. A decentralised structure can be motivating for employees.[1] This is because local branch or section managers will have more responsibility and authority to make decisions.[1]   [2]

5. There will be a greater pool of potential candidates[1] which could lead to the business recruiting and selecting a better candidate to the role.[1] / External candidates may bring a fresh approach / new experience from outside the company[1] which could offer new ideas and improvements.[1]   [2]

6. One benefit is that the training will be bespoke to the candidate[1] because they will be receiving training that is specific to their role / level of ability so they can learn the skills necessary to carry out their tasks.[1] / OJT is cheaper to provide[1] which would save the business costs.[1] / An individual can still offer some level of productivity[1] which would contribute to the growth and success of the business whilst training.[1]   [2]

7. **This question should be marked in accordance with the levels-based mark scheme on page 105.**

Having a motivated workforce will lower staff turnover reducing the number of employees leaving to rival airlines.[✔] Reduced staff turnover helps keep the cost of recruitment[✔] and training down.[✔] This is because they wouldn't have to recruit and train as many new staff constantly.[✔] This could help improve the profits for the budget airline.[✔]

A motivated employee is more likely to deliver a better customer experience for the passenger / customer.[✔] This would increase the likelihood of passengers writing a positive review about the airline.[✔] This would potentially boost the number of people that fly with the airline,[✔] increasing the company profit.[✔]   [4]

8.   **This question should be marked in accordance with the levels-based mark scheme on page 105.**

One benefit is that the aviation company is more likely to get candidates with the required skills to be effective pilots and cabin crew.[✔] This would allow the airline to provide the best in-flight service to its passengers.[✔] This would increase the satisfaction for the employee,[✔] increasing the likelihood they stay with the airline.[✔] / Meaning that customers will be happy with the quality of their flight experience,[✔] making them more likely to travel with the airline again.[✔]   [4]

9.   **This question should be marked in accordance with the levels-based mark scheme on page 106.**

Decision making is held by the few at the top of the hierarchy based at the airline's head office in London.[✔] They make decisions and then pass them down through the layers to pilots and cabin crew.[✔] This can be less effective with a longer chain of command[✔] because communication can be slower.[✔] It can also be less motivating for cabin crew, who don't have the authority to make their own decisions in quicker time.[✔] Lack of delegation may be one reason that many of them are leaving to work for rival airlines.[✔] This will mean that they have to recruit new cabin crew which can be expensive.[✔]

However, a narrower span of control is formed with a tall hierarchy[✔] which makes it easier for monitoring and on job training.[✔] More layers also offer greater opportunity for promotion[✔] which could be motivating for cabin crew,[✔] reducing absenteeism / staff turnover.[✔]   [6]

10. **This question should be marked in accordance with the levels-based mark scheme on page 105.**

The airline carries out induction training with pilots and cabin crew to ensure that they know what to do when in flight.[✔] This helps them to feel more comfortable in their new role.[✔] The airline's induction programme includes safety protocols and customer service essentials.[✔] This means that a cabin crew member will know how to keep passengers safe when they fly,[✔] therefore they will have a better flight experience / SkyLink will have a better safety record.[✔] As a result, passengers may be more likely to fly with SkyLink Express again.[✔] This will create customer loyalty for the airline and an improved reputation.[✔]   [6]

11. **This question should be marked in accordance with the levels-based mark scheme on page 105.**

One reason for introducing the zero contracts is that it may be better financially for the airline.[✔] This is because they will only be paying cabin crew when they actually work.[✔] This means that when they have fewer flights going / at off-peak times, they will reduce their costs as they will need fewer cabin crew members to work.[✔] This could help to improve the cash flow position of the airline.[✔]

Some staff may also welcome the flexibility this offers them[✔] as they can choose when to work at times convenient to them.[✔] However, introducing this may demotivate other staff.[✔] This is because other airlines may have more attractive financial packages on offer.[✔] As a result, more flight staff may leave the airline to work for rivals / insufficient staff may be available / want to work when there is higher demand.[✔] This could leave the airline with even fewer cabin crew to run the flights so it may lead to disruption or cancellation of flights.[✔] This would lead to passengers becoming frustrated,[✔] and purchasing flights with another airline.[✔]

In conclusion, it is crucial that the airline keeps costs low as it is operating on a tight budget and in a competitive market,[✔] so it's vital that prices are low.[✔] By introducing the zero hours, it will only pay for cabin crew when they are flying so therefore cost minimisation is achieved,[✔] allowing them to be competitively priced.[✔] However, whether this is successful will depend on the financial package offered when staff do fly.[✔] It must be sufficient to keep them motivated or they will simply leave.[✔]   [9]

1.   A – Cash cow.   [1]

2.   D – Maturity.   [1]

3.   Sales in Year 2 = 156,000 − 33,000 − 34,000 − 48,500 = £40,500[1]
Market share in Year 1 = (28,500 ÷ 141,000) × 100 = 20.21%[1]
Market share in Year 2 = (40,500 ÷ 156,000) × 100 = 25.96%[1]
Change in market share = 25.96 − 20.21 = 5.75%[1]   [4]

4.   The business can increase the price[1] because customers will be willing to pay more to get branded products as they perceive them to be higher quality.[1] / A strong brand is more memorable / recognisable[1] which makes them stand out in a crowded marketplace amongst buyers.[1] / It may be easier to recruit staff[1] because people are more attracted to a recognisable brand that they know and trust.[1] / Less spend on advertising is required[1] as people already know and trust the brand / see the brand name everywhere.[1] / A strong brand is more likely to be trusted[1] which increases loyalty.[1]   [2]

5.   One reason is because it will help to increase sales[1] because customers think the products are now better value for money so are more likely to purchase / because customers feel extra pressure to purchase before the end of the promotional period.[1]   [2]

6.   One reason is because they have a unique, or technically superior product that they are introducing so they can charge a high price,[1] therefore customers will be willing to pay more money to obtain the latest product.[1]   [2]

7. This question should be marked in accordance with the levels-based mark scheme on page 105.

One way the florist business could segment the market is by income.[✔] This is because they will have customers wishing to spend differing amounts of money on flowers depending on their disposable income.[✔] For example, they can create expensive lavish bouquets for those with larger budgets.[✔] Whereas they can offer their budget-friendly options for those on lower incomes.[✔]

Location may be used to target customers.[✔] This is because they will want them to live within a reasonable distance from the shop[✔] (or within the UK for e-commerce orders[✔]) for the delivery drivers to reach them before the flowers perish.[✔] This will also save costs on deliveries made further afield.[✔]   [4]

8. This question should be marked in accordance with the levels-based mark scheme on page 105.

It is important that the florist meets the needs of customers so they are satisfied.[✔] If customers are not satisfied with the quality of the bouquets or the level of customer service then they may leave negative reviews.[✔] This could tarnish the reputation of quality that the Turners have built up over the years / loyalty may decline.[✔] As a result customers may start to buy flowers from their rivals.[✔]   [4]

9. This question should be marked in accordance with the levels-based mark scheme on page 105.

The Turners will have wanted to conduct research in order to find out what the needs of the customers in the South of England were.[✔] They had originally started up in central London and the needs of customers there may be very different from customers in the rest of the south east.[✔] This will ensure that they provide bouquets and a level of service that customers want.[✔] This would ensure that new branches of the florist sold enough bouquets in order to break-even,[✔] meaning that the expansion would not run into financial difficulty,[1] ultimately resulting in the Turners making more profit from their expansion.[✔]

The Turners will have wanted to find out who their competitors are,[✔] what they offered[✔], and for what prices.[✔] This would provide them with an insight into where the gaps in the market are / what was not being offered.[✔] This would help to define a USP[✔] which would attract more customers / increase loyalty to the store.[✔] The success of the expansion would be more likely to be a success / profits would increase as a result over time.[✔]   [6]

10. This question should be marked in accordance with the levels-based mark scheme on page 105.

Introducing e-commerce allows the Turners to reach a wider customer base.[✔] Currently they are just located in the south east, limiting customers to those that can reach the florist.[✔] Using a website, customers located anywhere in the UK can view and purchase bouquets online.[✔] This will allow the Turner family to receive increased orders of flowers,[✔] even outside of normal store opening hours[✔] which will allow the business to receive more revenue,[✔] potentially increasing the amount of profit that the florist makes.[✔]   [6]

11. This question should be marked in accordance with the levels-based mark scheme on page 106.

By introducing a low-price range of bouquets, the Turner family will be targeting more of a mass market.[✔] This is because their flowers will be more affordable to a wider group of potential customers.[✔] This will mean that the florist will receive more sales,[✔] which will lead to a greater inflow of cash.[✔] An entry-level / low-budget bouquet would also provide a way for people with lower budgets to become a customer which could lead to sales of more expensive bouquets in the future.[✔] This would allow the Turners to have funds to be able to use for their move into e- and m-commerce.[✔]

However, introducing a low-price range of bouquets may lead to a deterioration of their exclusive image that they have built up over the years.[✔] This may lead to existing customers perceiving that the quality of the flowers has been reduced,[✔] meaning that they may be less likely to purchase a bunch of flowers from the Turners,[✔] which could ultimately result in less sales for the florist.[✔]

In terms of growing and moving into e-commerce, having more affordable bouquets is crucial if this venture is to be successful.[✔] However, whether they should or not might depend on how large the increase in customers is going to be.[✔] If the rise in customers is not sufficient to increase revenues, then clearly this would not be a good option for the Turners.[✔] If they can maintain their reputation for high quality and excellent customer service whilst introducing these low-priced bouquets then it can only be a good thing.[✔]   [9]

Section 3.6   Finance

1. C – Repayments on a bank loan.   [1]

2. C – Sale of assets.   [1]

3. Revenue = 600 × £12 = 7,200;[1] Total variable costs = 600 × 4.50 = £2,700;[1] Total cost = 3,200 + 2,700 = 5,900;[1]
   Profit = 7,200 – 5,900 = £1,300[1]   [4]

4.   A business can improve its cash flow is by agreeing an overdraft with the bank.[1] This will allow the business to be able to continue to withdraw money from their bank account even when it has a negative balance, so they can make any necessary payments.[1]

A business could apply for a loan.[1] This should increase the available cash amount to be able to pay for any additional costs / cover the expected period of shortfall in income.[1]

Unused assets could be sold[1] in order to raise sufficient finance to cover any period of shortfall.[1]

Agreements with trade suppliers could be renegotiated to increase the period of trade credit.[1] This would provide an extended period where cash outflows are reduced.[1]

A business owner could support the business with an injection of cash from their own funds / raised from friends and family.[1] This would provide a positive boost to cash flow which could help a business to get through a period where income was less than expected / outgoings were more than expected.[1]   [2]

5.   One benefit of using trade credit is that a business can purchase supplies without having to pay for them immediately.[1] This can enable the business to sell the products to the customers and receive payment from them before they need to pay the supplier.[1]   [2]

6.   Net profit for current year = 551m – 123m[1] = £428m[1] Net profit margin = (428 ÷ 5650) × 100[1] = 7.6%[1]   [4]

7.   Average rate of return = (Average return per annum ÷ Initial investment) × 100[1]
Answer = 8% / [4] Average return per annum = 120 ÷ 3[1] = £40m;[1] Average rate of return = (40 ÷ 500) × 100[1] = 8%[1]   [5]

8.   **This question should be marked in accordance with the levels-based mark scheme on page 105.**
StreamFlix should calculate the number of extra subscribers needed to break-even because it will show the streaming company whether investing in the women's football tournament is viable.[✔] This is because it will show whether the extra subscribers needed to cover the £500m investment is a realistic expectation.[✔] If it didn't conduct this financial analysis, the media company may end up in financial difficulty[✔] because they would invest a lot of money into the bid[✔] and may never receive sufficient income from subscribers and advertisers to make up the shortfall.[✔]   [4]

9.   **This question should be marked in accordance with the levels-based mark scheme on page 105.**
Those that control the rights to the women's international tournament will want to know that the digital company is financially secure.[✔] This is so they know that the digital firm will be able to have the necessary cash to pay for the rights to stream the matches.[✔] They will be able to see this from the statement of financial position.[✔] This is because it shows the level of cash that the business holds.[✔] The rights holders will also want to assess the profitability of the business, so they know they will not go out of business,[✔] which is shown in the income statement.[✔] The rights holders will see that in the current year, StreamFlix made a net profit of £428m.[✔] This will demonstrate to the rights holders that the streaming platform is in a strong financial position.[✔] / This could demonstrate to the rights holders that the streaming platform is unable to cover the additional costs of the rights through retained profit alone.[✔]   [6]

10.   **This question should be marked in accordance with the levels-based mark scheme on page 105.**
The overall revenue of the business increased over the year.[✔] The increase was by £942m / 20%.[✔] Costs of sales also increased over the period[✔] but only by £424m / 11%.[✔] This means that the company has become more profitable.[✔] The net profit was £428m compared to £103m.[✔] This demonstrates a strong performance over the year.[✔]   [6]

11.   **This question should be marked in accordance with the levels-based mark scheme on page 107.**
The advantage of using a bank loan to pay for the purchase of the rights to the women's football tournament is that no control is lost.[✔] The existing shareholders retain their same percentage ownership and current directors will remain in control.[✔] This means that they can continue on their current strategy of promoting sports to a diverse range of customers,[✔] which has proven successful, as last year's growth / net profit of £428 proves.[✔] However, using a bank loan will require the television entertainment company to pay the loan back with interest.[✔] This can hugely increase the fixed costs.[✔] This is particularly true for the streaming firm as they are looking to borrow around £500m.[✔] Increased costs may lead to the television streaming company having to increase the price of their subscriptions.[✔] This may mean that fewer people pay the monthly membership,[✔] therefore revenue from subscriptions may fall,[✔] harming their profits.[✔]

The advantage to the television media company of issuing shares is that relatively few costs will be incurred.[✔] This is because no repayments have to be made,[✔] which means that cash-flow is kept high.[✔] This will allow the steaming platform to continue to invest in the broadcasting rights of the major sporting events and latest programmes.[✔] Leading to a higher likelihood that more viewers will subscribe to the platform. Helping the business to increase future revenues from subscriptions.[✔] However, in issuing more shares, the streaming platform is susceptible to a takeover by a rival media company as anyone can buy the shares.[✔] If that happens, the business could take the media company in a different direction, perhaps removing the live sport element, which subscribers may not initially like[✔] and therefore they may choose to cancel their subscription as a result.[✔] Leading to potential failure of the business.[✔]

Overall, I think that taking out a loan will be the best option for the streaming platform. Although it costs more as interest has to be paid, the potential extra revenue they could gain from broadcasting a huge sporting event is worth the risk.[✔] This is because not only will they gain extra revenue from subscribers but also from advertisers who will want their products advertised during the live steams.[✔] However, my decision is dependent on the rate of interest charged.[✔] If the rate is high, then it may erode the extra £120m that they expect to receive over the next three years.[✔] If this is the case, then selling shares may be better.[✔]   [12]

LEVELS-BASED MARK SCHEMES FOR EXTENDED RESPONSE QUESTIONS

Questions that require extended writing use mark bands. The whole answer will be marked together to determine which mark band it fits into and which mark should be awarded within the mark band.

Explain questions

Level	Marks	Description
2	3–4	Sound understanding and application of the topics. • Applies knowledge and understanding to the context sufficiently. • A sound understanding of one or more business concepts and issues.
1	1–2	Basic understanding and application of the topics. • Applies basic knowledge and understanding to the context. • A basic understanding of one or more business concepts.
0	0	Nothing written worthy of credit.

Analyse questions

Level	Marks	Description
3	5–6	Detailed analysis of topics based on the context. • Business areas are fully analysed. • Applies knowledge and understanding to the context sufficiently.
2	3–4	Sound analysis of topics based on the context. • Business areas are partially analysed. • Applies some knowledge and understanding to the context.
1	1–2	Basic analysis of topics based on the context. • Basic analysis of business areas. • Basic knowledge and understanding is applied to the context.
0	0	Nothing written worthy of credit.

Recommend questions

Level	Marks	Description
3	7–9	Detailed analysis and evaluation of topics based on the context. • Sustained line of reasoning, which is coherent, relevant and substantiated with a focused conclusion that is fully justified. • Business areas are fully analysed. • Applies knowledge and understanding to the context sufficiently.
2	3–6	Sound analysis and evaluation of topics based on the context. • A line of reasoning, with a conclusion that has some justification. • Business areas are partially analysed. • Applies some knowledge and understanding to the context.
1	1–3	Basic analysis and evaluation of topics based on the context. • Basic line of reasoning with a conclusion. • Basic analysis of business areas. • Basic knowledge and understanding to the context.
0	0	Nothing written worthy of credit.

Level	Marks	Description
4	10–12	Developed, integrated analysis and evaluation of topics with sustained judgement based on context. • An integrated line of reasoning, which is coherent, relevant, with a conclusion. The area which has been impacted on the most has been fully justified. • Interdependent nature of business areas is fully analysed. • Applies knowledge and understanding to the context and successfully draws together several functional areas of business.
3	7–9	Detailed analysis and evaluation of topics based on the context. • A line of reasoning, which is coherent, relevant, with a conclusion that is justified. • Different business areas are analysed independently or the interdependent nature of business areas is partially analysed. • Applies knowledge and understanding to the context and starts to draw together several functional areas of business.
2	3–6	Sound analysis and evaluation of topics in isolation of their interdependence based on the context. • A line of reasoning, with a conclusion that has some justification. • One business area is analysed independently. • Applies some knowledge and understanding to the context.
1	1–3	Basic generic discussion of topics. • A basic understanding of business concepts in isolation. • A basic understanding of one or more business concepts. • Partial relevance to the question.
0	0	Nothing written worthy of credit.

INDEX

FORMULAE

Revenue	Selling price × Number of units sold
Total variable costs	Variable cost per unit × Number of units sold
Total costs	Fixed costs + Variable costs
Profit	Revenue − Total costs
Cost per unit	Total costs ÷ Number of units sold
Margin of safety	Actual output − Break even output
Net cash flow	Total receipts − Total payments
Closing balance	Opening balance + Net cash flow
Total assets	Non-current assets + Current assets
Net assets	(Non-current assets + Current assets) − (Current liabilities + Non-current liabilities)
Gross profit	Revenue − Cost of sales
Operating profit	Gross profit − Overheads
Net profit	Operating profit − Tax and interest
Gross profit margin	(Gross profit ÷ Revenue) × 100
Net profit margin	(Net profit ÷ Revenue) × 100
ARR	(Average return per annum ÷ cost of investment) × 100
Percentage change	(Change in figures ÷ Original figure) × 100
Average	Total of all the individual values ÷ The number of values in the set

You may have to demonstrate your basic quantitative skills as well as potentially being asked to use business calculations. This could include calculating the percentage change between two figures or calculating the average of a set of data.

You will not be provided with formulae in the exam.

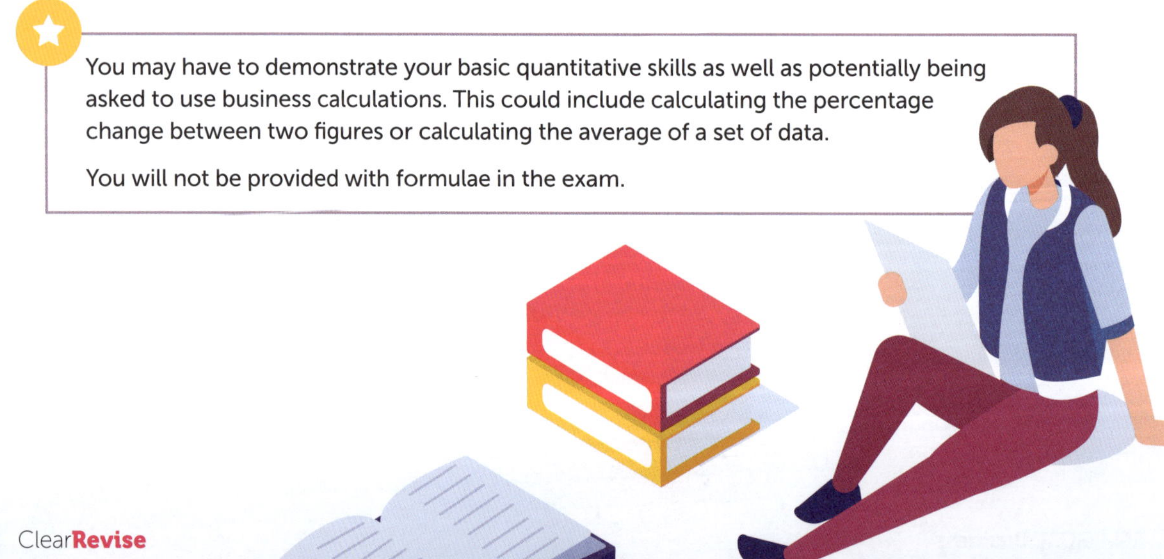

EXAMINATION TIPS

When you practice exam questions, work out your approximate grade using the following table. This table has been produced using a rounded average of past examination series for this GCSE. Be aware that boundaries vary by a few percentage points either side of those shown.

Grade	9	8	7	6	5	4	3	2	1
Boundary	74%	69%	63%	56%	49%	42%	31%	20%	8%

1. Read the questions carefully as some students give answers to questions they think are appearing rather than the actual question.

2. In calculation questions, marks may be awarded for workings out if the final answer is incorrect. Make sure to show your working in case you make a mistake and the answer is incorrect. Workings also help you check your own answers at the end of an exam.

3. Calculation questions account for a large proportion of marks on each paper; make sure you have learned the formulae.

4. Try to not repeat the question in the first line of your response. It will not score you any marks and simply wastes your time. Avoid losing marks by not finishing the paper.

5. When explaining your points, use clear connectives to show that you are developing the point you have made and not moving onto a separate point. These connectives include; *'thus'*, *'therefore'*, *'this means that'*, *'this leads to'*, *'because'* and *'as a consequence'*. This demonstrates your skills of analysis which are assessed in all longer written questions.

6. Ensure that you include the context in any question that contains a business' name, even in the shorter questions. Many students forget this and throw away easy marks that could make the difference between grades.

7. All questions are marked according to their Assessment Objectives. Each question starts with a command word. Make sure you fully understand what each command word requires you to do. Reading the command verbs at the start of this book will help you with this.

Good luck!